The Wages of Sin

Miguel A. Valembrun Jr.

Copyright © 2020 Miguel A. Valembrun Jr.

All rights reserved.

ISBN: 978-1-950773-02-2

DEDICATION

To my God and King who created this world and sent His son to die for all sins so that anyone who believes in Him will not perish but have everlasting life. LORD, I thank you for your salvation, for without the death of Jesus upon the cross, not one soul would ever have the hope of eternal life with you.

CONTENTS

	INTRODUCTION	Pg 5
1	Chapter one	Pg 17
2	Chapter two	Pg 29
3	Chapter three	Pg 34
4	Chapter four	Pg 42
5	Chapter five	Pg 52
6	Chapter six	Pg 64
7	Chapter seven	Pg 69
8	Chapter eight	Pg 73
9	Chapter nine	Pg 86
10	Chapter ten	Pg 91
11	Chapter eleven	Pg 102
12	Chapter twelve	Pg 108
13	Chapter thirteen	Pg 111
14	Chapter fourteen	Pg 124
15	Chapter fifteen	Pg 130
16	Chapter sixteen	Pg 140

INTRODUCTION

From the serpent's lie in the garden of Eden to our present day, the world has experienced a paradigm shift that caused it to turn away from the knowledge of God. Now, as the Bible foretold, society worships creation instead of the Creator. Major sciences (such as biology, psychology, geology, and astrophysics) exemplify humanity's foreshadowed infatuation with the product (the entirety of creation). Furthermore, they reveal our indifference toward the Maker. Rather than give glory to the one who made all, we study His work and deny His existence. The Bible also foretold that people of this world would profess themselves to be wise and exchange the truth of God for a lie.

Many deceptions in this world lead us away from the truth of God. They distract and fool those who do not understand or appreciate the fact that they are fearfully and wonderfully _made_. In this book, we will explore both the spiritual and physical aspects of our fascinating composition, the nature of reality, how sin separates us from the love of God, and what God did to reconcile a sinful world to Himself. I have not written this book from the abundance of my own intellect (because I was also blind), and apart from God, I am foolish. Instead, I share with you a wealth of truth, which through God's grace and revelation, I am now blessed to behold. His truth has the power to change lives and set people free.

Like most of the world, you are a prisoner of deception. You have lived in that imprisonment for much of your life. The extent to which you have been bound may be more severe than I suspect, but I know deep down, dear reader, you want to be free. This world is seriously flawed, an unfortunate fact I am sure you know well, but it isn't because of racists, fascists, communists, feminists, white supremacists, the left, right, or any of a thousand plus factions we can name. No. This world is messed up because of you; yes, but it is not just because of you—it is also messed up because of me, —and because of everyone else born into it.

You see, everyone who has ever lived has sinned and fallen short of God's glorious standard. The Bible tells us this straightforwardly. We have strayed away. Most people hear that and prefer to plug their ears like impolite children. They do not want to hear that they are not innately good, but instead, prefer to think that the sins they commit are not hurting anyone. Some like to believe the remedy is in themselves as if they are God's gift to the world, or as though they can find divinity and worthiness of eternal life within themselves. They fail to see the hideousness of sin and how even the smallest lies lead to mistrust, the smallest thefts to insecurity, the smallest acts of aggression to fear and trauma, or the smallest acts of betrayal to heartbreak. Oddly, many of them have been wronged by those who also thought 'they weren't hurting anyone.'

"How could she lie to me?" "How could he break my heart?" "How could they betray me?" Even sins which the world considers trivial (like a white lie) can result in tremendous damage. For instance, in

THE WAGES OF SIN

1955, a woman and some false witnesses said a 14-year-old black boy had whistled at her. That story enraged some members of the "white community" (one of this world's many factions), and the boy was lynched over what was later revealed to have been a lie. Perhaps, at the time, she had no idea of how widespread and devastatingly ramified her lie would become. The murderers were acquitted, and this event and others of similar nature became the spark and fuel of the Civil Rights movement of the 1960s.

To this day, tensions exist between the black and white communities, along with much of the prejudice and injustice that led to them. The basis for these tensions is multifaceted. Part of it has to do with black history (how black people were brought to this country and what they endured); part of it has to do with the kindled feelings of unforgiveness and even hatred towards the oppressors and their offspring. Still another part has to do with the apparent apathy to the cries of the oppressed. This is a multifaceted issue, but one of the things most people have overlooked is the lie that was so subtle it hid in plain sight. This little lie, so seemingly harmless, yet evidently malicious, was the very one that made it possible for some to better justify their racism and hatred. It was the lie that we were not at all created after God's image but evolved after billions of random events which conveniently and magically aligned themselves over billions of years. This evolutionary force finally made a few people superior to everyone else. The people of the world bought this lie even if they did so subconsciously—but lies cannot stand up to the light of truth.

God deliberately designed us after His image. Evolution, however, merely created an accepted justification for slavery, inequality, and the exclusion of black people from the "self-evident **truth**" that all human beings were **_created_** equal. According to the United States' Declaration of Independence, it was **self-evident** (or obvious) that human beings were created by God and endowed with certain "unalienable rights." Since then, however, God has been slowly pushed out of our collective worldview. White slave owners using evil powers of coercion and manipulation, as well as tactics outlined in the Willie Lynch letters, lowered black slaves to the existential level of animals.

Moreover, they had the audacity to remove entire sections of what would later be called "the Slave Bible," sections that would have empowered black slaves in the knowledge that the wickedness of their masters would not go unpunished by God. Not even He forces His way upon others even though He can. Instead, He gives us the power to choose whether to obey His laws, which leads to life and joy, or disobey and bring death and condemnation upon ourselves.

The human heart selfishly desires comfort and advantages, often at the expense of others. To that end, anything that does not promote one's interest constitutes what we call a *conflict of interest.* Many issues plague this world, and they begin with the sin in our hearts. Friction and tension between individuals, factions, nations, etc. are the evidence and manifestations of conflicting interests. The reality we perceive is a complex matrix of interactions (with human interactions being the most consequential). Out of the massive horde of humanity, **not <u>one</u> person** has ever been infallible (except Christ Jesus, who was God in a human, —killable form). While perfection is an ideal many strive for, we cannot achieve it on our own! We need to seek God, His righteousness and forgiveness, and then adhere to His standards. People lie, steal, and cheat. It is in our nature! We break hearts, betray, and disappoint others all the time. Some people demonstrate higher —or even extreme —levels of inner darkness than others, but make no mistake, we were all born sinners. Only God can perfect us through a continuous (life-long) process of inner healing, cleansing, and restoration!

It is said that hurt people, hurt people. We see this when a heart-broken individual breaks another's heart or when someone who was given a venereal disease from another whom they had trusted, knowingly spreads it to others. Dear reader, sometimes the truth must hurt us first before it ever heals us. Not one person on earth is *good* by nature. For all have sinned and fallen short of the glory of God. If that fact hurts, well, it should. Flattery only scratches itching ears and does not help people face the truth of the brokenness and darkness within. Daring to think of one's self as good is boastful and arrogant. Slamming this book shut because we want to remain in denial will not help either.

Anyone who thinks they are good is engaging in moral relativism, which is like determining who among a group of people drew the straightest line. Instead of using a straight edge, these relativists visually compare everyone's crooked lines to find the straightest one. They ignore the most excellent standard (God Himself) against which their imperfection can be gauged and rationalize their misdeeds using fallacies such as "necessary evil." They raise themselves on pedestals, failing to realize that through all the lies they have ever told (big or small), and all the wrongs committed (stealing, lusting, mistreating others, etc.), no matter how decent they claimed to be, they were demonstrating their involvement in the world's deepest and most elusive problem,—SIN.

You see, society is like that movie "The Gremlins." It is full of imperfect little creatures, some of whom are perceivably worse than others. Even so, all of them wreak havoc upon their world, with some only being more extreme than others. Many consider themselves to be "good," basing their self-assessment on the world's definition of "goodness," which to this day is merely a corrupted rendition of the standards God gave to man. The same people who do their "good deed of the day" can also show their ugly side. For instance, impatience, materialism, and pride are three qualities of entitled people, and anyone can be or become entitled (even those who give to the poor). Many people who do good things often have foul mouths, uttering profanities, or using vulgar names against others. Furthermore, they may instigate conflict with obscene gestures and body language, or express unpleasant attitudes toward others. Many even consider it endearing to jokingly call their friends lewd names, and those same "good people" are often easily angered, lustful, greedy, disobedient to parents, inconsiderate toward elders, apathetic to the needy, and or violent...etc. Not one person is naturally good overall.

We are all part of a chaotic and self-destructive world in which our internal conflicts with sin aggregate into our collective travail. Moreover, our lives are a microcosm of the world's self-destructive pattern. When we zoom in to an individual scale (to examine" the trees" as it were, instead of "the forest"), we see that people harm their bodies by overindulging in food, drugs, sexual immorality, comfort, etc. Individuals also hurt others through selfish acts. Unrighteous thoughts and actions resulting from lust, greed, jealousy, and untamed desires for physical pleasure are all things that can bring about conflict. Conflict can trigger anger, which can lead to hate and violence. Violence, in turn, often results in fear and leads to self-sustaining cycles whereby fear created by violent encounters perpetuates a spirit of vengeance leading to more violence, trauma, anger, hatred, unforgiveness, retaliation. Repeat. As we zoom out, we begin to notice that *macroscopically*, neighborhoods, cities, states, regions, countries, continents, and then the whole world reflect our own internal brokenness and imperfection.

To those who say society is the problem, I would challenge their statement with this. Who comprises society? Are we not all part of it? Have we not learned about groupthink, demographic and market trends, cultural forces, and other related topics from our social studies? Those topics indicate that factions act as one entity with singular mindsets and agendas. Furthermore, the mental profile of the average individual within a sect matches the cognitive profile of the whole. Each individual is, therefore, an adequate sample or representation of his or her group's *general* way of thinking. For instance, the unanimous belief that sexuality is fluid, and that homosexuality should be viewed no differently than heterosexuality unites the LGBTQ community. If we were to take one individual out of that group, for a study, his or her general way of thinking would reflect the general viewpoint of their group. Likewise, the same person who watches porn (for instance) is part of a broader market of people who are motivated by similar lustful drives. They crave sexual gratification even at their expense, for there are indeed side effects of watching porn. Indirectly, they also affect the well-being of the "actors" whether they thought they were hurting anyone or not.

Like any other industry, the forces of supply and demand are at work in the Sex Industry. Because of our lusts and sexual immorality, countless people, mostly women and even young girls, have been trafficked and or sexually abused before they ever entered the industry, of which pornography is a subset. Those who drive the demand for a greater supply of porn are not shouting for it in the streets. They are "voting" for it with their silent web-surfing. They may not be labeled as "sex offenders" by human beings who often try and redefine what is morally acceptable or **offensive** and what's not, but God sees them as such. A surprising fact most people may have never dared to consider up to this point is that the vast majority of sex offenders are not "registered." Instead, we cross paths with these criminals daily. Secret porn-addicts keep the sex and human trafficking industry in business, and once upon a time, I was among them. However, God loved me too much to lose me to it, and I began to love and appreciate what He wanted for my life. Dear reader, He loves you also. It is not because I am naturally moral that I no longer struggle with this sin.

THE WAGES OF SIN

The Bible says our waking thoughts are evil. I no longer struggle with porn because the LORD is my redeemer, and I have replaced my desires for it with a desire to seek Him. He can save and transform the lives of all who believe and **choose** to remain in Him.

Life is a constant battle over the eternal destiny of our souls. If we are not careful, we can backslide and forfeit God's promise of salvation. That is why the scriptures say, "work out your own salvation with fear and trembling," for all sins are crimes worthy of punishment to the LORD. Though He is inconceivably gracious and forgiving, intentional sins offend Him as a child who rushes into mud would upset the parent who had washed her only moments before. Most people compare sin, and indeed, some sins are more impactful than others, but they are all worthy of the same punishment in God's sight. Additionally, many people deem certain sins as "harmless" and "okay." Perhaps prisons are not large enough for everyone and every crime, but hell is enormous enough to accommodate all newcomers.

Though God is compassionate and gracious, slow to anger, and ready to forgive all iniquity, transgression, and sin, by no means will He allow the guilty to go unpunished. Just so we are clear, He does not want to condemn anyone to hell. That is why He made a way to escape the horrendous fate we all work toward (when we live in sin). Sadly, many people (enslaved by their carnal desires) will neglect the great salvation and eternally doom themselves in the process. Those who work iniquity will be there. Those who keep silent about sin or worse, promote it, show where their allegiance lies.

Everyone has fallen short and contributed to the groupthink (and action) of this devastated world. We have earned the ultimate penalty, which is endless suffering for the infinite havoc we would wreak if the end were never to come. Fortunately (for those who grow tired of wickedness), God promises the end **will** come. Those who accept Christ and the sacrifice He made will be shown mercy, for they are choosing to glorify the One who loved them since the moment He imagined making them. They will worship Him in their speech, their conduct, the way they love others, and in their acknowledgment of Him (instead of indifference toward Him), and they will dwell in a world free from sin and suffering. You see, creation has been defiled by countless lies, murders, rapes, thefts, etc., and those who dare to partake in sin with the mentality that there's no harm in it, continue to dip their hands in the blood this world has shed. Worse, since Christ's blood also was spilled by this world, being of infinite preciousness, those who choose sin will have to pay for His blood drop for drop. While Jesus' blood, which was shed on the cross, spiritually redeems those who accept Him as Lord, it incriminates those who choose to continue their lives of sin. They will be counted among those whose lies, hatred, greed, cowardice, inaction, etc. led to the murder of our risen Savior.

If you feel troubled to your core, then it is evidence that *inwardly, you know all I have written is true, but you may be tempted to deny it outwardly*! Please do not do this. As flawed as you are, dear reader, and as much as I have spoken against your flawed nature, I have not, and will not attack your value, for you are immeasurably precious to God! He loves us all so much that it is impossible to find a word that even comes close to describing the extent to which He does. If you have ever heard something like this from someone who let you down, the fact that they disappointed you has not invalidated God's love for you! Anyone who fell short of your expectations merely displayed the human predisposition to fail short at least once. God, however, will never let you down, and I confidently declare this because He has not disappointed me, nor anyone who has ever sincerely trusted Him.

Without Christ, the lost are drowning in the seas of their iniquity. If some begin thinking to themselves, "Well, I splash around better than everyone else, so I'll be the last to go under," won't those proud ones also drown if no one saves them? There is only one way out of escaping the wages of sin, and it is not by comparing ourselves to others; nor through meditation and inner reflection, though the Bible does talk about meditating on God's words. No, the way to eternal life is in accepting God's salvation through Jesus, the Messiah. He has reached out for us to grab hold of His hand. We can fail. We have been doing exactly that on our own, and consistently, but He cannot fail!

God will not let us drown if we sincerely turn to Him. Once He has us in His hands, He will not fumble with us. However, without His life-saving help, no one can or ever will be able to stand in His perfectly holy and righteous presence. It is prideful and wishful thinking to imagine otherwise. Thinking we are just naturally good and do not need God drives us to secretly seek the approval and adoration of others as we feign humility, but true humility exalts God. True humility is shown when we realize we need help, and apart from God, we can do nothing.

God created each of us with a special purpose. We may be fallen creatures, yes, but we bear the image of a forgiving God who just wants to raise us above our former glory, which we forfeited in the garden of Eden. He wants to do this so we can dwell in righteousness with Him. We, however, have a part to play. As creatures of free agency, we must use our freedom of choice and humble ourselves before Him. We must accept Him as the glorious and perfectly righteous, holy, and loving God He is, and we must accept His son Christ Jesus who restored us to fellowship with Him.

We are not insignificant! Nothing we do is trivial! Nothing can separate us from the love of God, although our choices can separate us from enjoying a wonderful relationship with Him. God loves us despite our shortcomings and desires to do good things in, through, and for us. Without Him, however, we can only work iniquity, and the Bible tells us, "the wages of sin is death."

CHAPTER 1
The Living Soul

After Adam and Eve ate from the forbidden tree of the knowledge of good and evil, sin and death spread like wildfire throughout their world. Every new human being born into this world would acquire their fallen nature and mortality. They would be unable to please the LORD through their efforts alone, for the LORD God is Holy.

Sin begins in our thoughts. Every evil deed originates as the very thought of it. After eating from the Knowledge Tree, human beings gained the ability to contemplate mischief and wickedness. We learned to entertain immoral thoughts brought about by jealousy, lust, greed, impatience, arrogance, and so on. At times, we even act upon them. This capacity comes from the darkness naturally found in each of us. No one taught us how to speak our first lie, covet things that are not ours, or where (within our hearts) to find the harmful emotion called "jealousy." One day, we just lied. At some point during our early development, most of us stole something, knowing that had we simply asked for that something, the answer would most likely have been "No."

The more we run from the truth of God, the deeper we tend to drift through the gradients of darkness. We have heard stories of people who "lost control" or "snapped" and behaved disgracefully as a result. Even in the heat of the moment, actions always begin as thoughts. Before someone tells a lie, he or she must first *think* of the deception and figure out how to deliver it. Likewise, whenever someone steals, their imagination *always* precedes the act. Imaginations improve the more we use them, and if we are using ours for unethical reasons, we become more adept at sinning.

In the following chapter, we will follow the account of Cain and Abel (Adam and Eve's most well-known sons). Before we get there, however, I would first like to explain the relationships between the spirit, brain, mind, heart, body, soul, and the will, because we must understand what they are and how they interact with one another. Understanding those aspects of ourselves (in a way in which we had not before) is fundamental to comprehending how we interact with our world for better or worse.

The Spirit

The spirit of a person by itself is his or her innermost consciousness. Your spirit is "the real you," dear reader, as mine is the real me. Like everything else, it originated from God. The spirit is invisible, even to its person. When we look in a mirror, none of us can see our spirit. We simply see the shell that houses it. The spirit tends to be most influenced by what it exposes itself to the most. For instance, if one mostly surrounds himself with evil thoughts and desires, his spirit will most likely become evil. If he surrounds himself with knowledge and understanding, he will probably become wise; and if he immerses himself in confusion and false notions, then his spirit will likely become confused. That is a simple model of how our spirits develop individually. Each person exposes himself or herself to different experiences at different times and developmental stages. Still, one who sincerely seeks God inevitably approaches Godliness while one who seeks out sin instead remains sinful.

The Brain

The brain itself is the physical organ that *transmits* and *translates* information to the body. It interprets data received from the external environment via the vast network of sensors organized throughout the body. According to an article called "THE GIFTED MIND Learning to Think," published by Sylvia Cadena Smith in 2014, "Research shows that the human brain processes **400 billion bits** of information per second."! Although we know we have powerful processing capabilities, somewhere deep down, we also know *we are **not** our brains*. We do not consciously regulate our temperatures, heartbeats, nor even the smallest automatic processes within our bodies. We (as in our consciousness, awareness, and identity) exist *alongside* the brain. If one dared to hold their breath to end their life, they would be utterly disappointed. We are not able to induce death by the sheer will to "shut down," neither are we supposed to. The spirit of life is the breath within us, which only God should reclaim in **His** time, for God designed the brain to maintain all biorhythmic activities to the best of its ability even while unconscious.

The Mind

We often use the terms brain and mind interchangeably, but there *is* a big difference between them! Simply put, the mind is entirely nonphysical. It encapsulates the entirety of thought, consciousness, personality, conscience, and identity, all of which are invisible and intangible. The mind is not the brain, but it **is** the brain's computing power harnessed and combined with the awareness of the spirit. The mind also consists of the thoughts and desires of the heart (which, by the by, has its own neural network according to several late 20th century discoveries). According to an article published on www.heartmath.org:

"the heart has a complex neural network that is sufficiently extensive to be characterized as a brain on the heart. The heart-brain, as it is commonly called, or intrinsic cardiac nervous system, is an intricate network of complex ganglia, neurotransmitters, proteins, and support cells, the same as those of the brain in the head. The heart-brain's neural circuitry enables it to act independently of the cranial brain to learn, remember, make decisions and even feel and sense."

When the Bible refers to the heart, it personifies it and expresses that it has thoughts of its own. For instance, Mark 7:21-23 says, "For from within, out of the heart of man, come evil thoughts, sexual immorality, theft, murder, adultery, coveting, wickedness, deceit, sensuality, envy, slander, pride, foolishness. All these evil things come from within, and they defile a person." Genesis 6:5 says, "The Lord saw that the wickedness of man was great in the earth and that every ***intention of the <u>thoughts of his heart</u>*** was only evil continually."

I am utterly amazed at the Bible for having spoken on things thousands of years before man could fully comprehend them, or ever discover evidence to support them. Much like the first surgical operation that took place in the garden of Eden (before the human mind could ever contemplate such a feat), God showed that his knowledge preceded ours and will always supersede it. He taught us that the heart could think, not just "feel." This spirit-heart-brain dynamic is what we call the mind. It can also be considered as "the inner soul."

The Body

Our bodies are some of the most advanced machinery *ever* designed! Though most often, people associate one's identity with the physical shell they can see, we are not the body we occupy, just as we are not our brains. The body is merely a shell. We are instead, invisible spirits dwelling within the flesh. Thus, the spirit is like the driver of a car who wills the vehicle to move simply by shifting gears, turning the wheel, and pressing the gas pedal. The driver of an automobile does not directly control the cylinders, fuel injectors, fuel pump, motors, air intake, alternator, and most of the processes that enable modern vehicles to drive down a road. He simply guides the car down a compatible route and calls it "driving." Most people do not require in-depth knowledge of the inner workings of an automobile to use it. They just turn it on and move by interacting with the steering wheel, gear shift, and pedals. Likewise, the bodies of living organisms are incredibly complex machines. Most people are unaware of all the intricate processes taking place within their bodies, yet they understand the rudiments of operating their "spirit-driven machines." They live out their lives, rarely appreciating sincerely how fearfully and wonderfully God made them.

Much like the machines we build, our bodies run on battery technology (found in cellular mitochondria). Additionally, we run on both electricity and chemistry (hence the term "electrochemical"). We have a plethora of sensors (such as advanced light and sound detection, accelerometry, etc.), motors (as in "gross motor skills"), and other remarkable features and functions! We are exceedingly impressive beyond what we could ever design or even conceive, and yet in our oblivion to God, we fail to grasp the majesty of our existence. How tragic!

The will

Our will is the intention of our spirit. It is manifested through physical action once we have committed to that action. The machine (or mechanism) through which a human being interfaces with this world is his or her body—and here is how it works:

Our spirit interacts with the physical world by first communicating with the brain. Recall that the brain and spirit interaction is what we refer to as the mind. The brain is merely our central processing unit. If the will of our spirit is to throw an object, the brain's job is to calculate variables such as direction, trajectory, and environmental forces like wind. We can consider the mind (or spirit-brain) as a single unit that desires (or intends) to throw an object. From there, the brain transmits electrochemical signals to the physical body to achieve the objective—or will of the spirit.

- The eyes see the intended target.
- If the target is moving, the brain continues to compute possible scenarios.
- The arm and hand that holds the object get ready for an impulse from the brain.
- Once the *mind* commits, the object will be thrown following ones **will** to throw it.

The Soul

Now the soul is the combination of brain, mind, and spirit. It can—depending on context—include the body as one complete being. That is because consciousness involves the senses (which are mostly somatic).

Most people, when speaking about the soul, refer to the invisible qualities, the hidden desires, unspoken thoughts, habits, mannerisms, etcetera. However, the soul is the byproduct of a bond between the breath of life (the spirit which is from God) and the flesh:

And the LORD God formed man of the dust of the ground, and breathed into his nostrils the breath of life, and man became a living soul. - Genesis 2:7

Human beings *are* living souls that consist of intangible (and tangible) aspects. Souls can grow and change with time, and through each experience and decision they make.

Decisions are like tree branches that divide into infinite possibilities. As time passes by, we generally become more fixed in our ways, much like a fully grown tree, which has become less movable. Each soul develops distinctly because of the different decisions that one can make as well as the results that follow each choice.

As an analogy, when we identify a tree, we can tell it apart from other trees (even of the same species) not only by the type of fruit it bears (if it is fruit-bearing) but also by how it has developed. For instance, trees can grow to different heights, different widths around their trunks; they can have varying amounts of branches, leaf counts, fruits, etc. These differences are like the individuality of each soul.

Contrary to popular belief, we **can** see the "soul" in its all-encompassing context! It expresses bitterness, stress, sorrow, etc. as the 'countenance upon one's face.' The soul is also the ultimate decision-maker. It either chooses to act upon the impulses of the brain or to override them. When I decide to do something, people see my body doing it. Deep down, they know that it is not just my body acting; neither is it merely my brain but my invisible consciousness (the spirit they cannot see within the body which they can see).

One of the greatest and most common misconceptions about our brains is that it makes our decisions. This came from secular approaches to understanding human behavior. The standard psychiatric understanding of the brain reflects an inadequate perception of the human being (its essence and what it means to **be** *human*). It does not consider that a fundamental element of our composition is the spirit within us. Instead, modern psychiatry falsely surmises that our brains control us. And it would seem that way, wouldn't it? The brain, however, is merely a processing unit for sensory inputs and responsive outputs. It computes, transmits, and receives information. Therefore, the higher consciousness (which is the spirit) can override suggestions sent by the brain. For instance, my brain can tell me I am hungry, but I can choose to fast despite the impulse. If I decide to fast, then my spirit (which may have desired that I practice self-control) overrides my brain.

My mind (or my inner soul) is now conflicted with the unanimity of my flesh. On the one hand, my spirit wants to fast; on the other hand, my flesh wants to eat, but the spirit-side must overcome the flesh-side for me to fast. If my desires change, I may experience a change of mind (not of brain). Remember, the mind is the processing power of the brain, <u>combined</u> with the awareness of the spirit. If my flesh-side (the unity of brain and body) overcomes my spirit, then I will eat. If not, I will fast. My soul (or my entire being), therefore, cooperates in deciding either way.

My brain may continue to *remind* me that my body is hungry. Still, my soul is the overall decision-maker (working through complete submission of the spirit to the flesh, agreement with spirit and flesh, compromise between the two, or total dominance of the spirit over the flesh). In the hunger scenario, my soul decides *when* and how to act to satisfy my want for food, for it considers the hunger signals sent by my brain as well as the desire of my spirit. Our brains do not **make us** eat or do anything else for that matter.

During decision-making, the brain transforms the soul's will into physical action. Here, we can see that the soul (spirit-body duo) can communicate its intention to the body (via the brain). If the desired outcome requires a physical influence on the environment, then the brain will translate the will of the soul to the body, which will then act as needed. *That* is how intangible spirits interact with physical environments.

The brain is one big module for transmitting and receiving information. The flesh, which has a massive array of sensors (visual ones, auditory, olfactory, haptic, etc.), carries hundreds of billions of bits of information per second to the brain for processing. It computes and organizes light, shadow, colors, volume, bass, treble, pressure, weight, relative speed, humidity, and much more! When it has finished processing the data, the soul (or the entire consciousness in question) "sees," "hears," "feels," etc. Thus far, we have established that the soul not only transmits information to the brain but also receives from it. In this manner, the brain is an intermediary between the spirit and the body. To summarize, the brain is a central processing unit within the flesh-covered machine. That is all!

The words "soul" and "spirit" have often been interchanged just as brain and mind often are, but they are not the same. For as long as God has assigned a spirit to a body, it is the element that brings life to the otherwise dead body. Before God blew life into Adam, he was a lifeless sculpture. The breath of life was the final ingredient that vivified Adam and transformed him into what the Bible calls a "living soul" (according to Genesis 2:7). A soul can only exist when God assigns a spirit to inhabit a body.

The word "animate" comes from the Latin "animatus," the past participle of the verb "animare," which means "to fill with breath" or as we better understand it, "to fill with life." Breath itself translates to "spiritus" in Latin, the root of words like "respire" (to breathe), or, more obviously, "spirit!" Therefore, animating humankind involved God filling each person with a *spirit* (the "Spirit of Life," which must be a "living" spirit)! Until God breathed into Adam's flesh, he did not become a living soul.

The Bible tells us the spirit is from God. It is the "breath" that returns to Him when people die (Ecclesiastes 12:7). Therefore, the spirit is (in a sense) as an intelligent battery of some sort. Again, the man did not come to life until God installed this battery and its consciousness, for the spirit contained the power needed to spark and sustain life.

The soul is sophisticated. The human *being* consists of the spirit component (the consciousness), and the flesh component (the machine we call the human body). The body is "driven" by the spirit within but managed by the squishy matter we call "the brain" (which merely receives and transmits information). Finally, we get to the importance of blood. It fills the spaces within our bodies to serve as the conduit which marries the spirit and flesh).

CHAPTER 2
Rivalry

The story of Cain and Abel teaches us about the irreversible damage that can occur when we succumb to darkness within ourselves. It is in this account of the Bible that we discover how sin rules wherever the power of temptation breaks the willingness to do well.

The Bible says that Adam and Eve knew each other (they were sexually intimate), and the first two children Eve gave birth to were sons named Cain and Abel. Both Cain and Abel grew up with the knowledge of the LORD God. Cain became a farmer while Abel became a shepherd. One day, both brothers made offerings to the LORD. Cain offered fruits from the ground while Abel offered some of the firstlings of his flock. God accepted Abel's offering, but not Cain's. As a result, Cain became bitter against His brother.

And the LORD said unto Cain, "Why are you angry? And why is your countenance fallen? If you do well, shall you not be accepted? And if you do not do well, sin lies at the door. And you shall be its desire, and you must rule over it." - (Genesis 4:6-7)

God was trying to tell Cain something to the following effect:

'Why are you angry? I am always fair. I do not accept one and reject another for no reason! Cain, dear human, you did not do well, yet you are allowing your anger to consume you! Be careful, child, because when you do not do well, you are doing wrong, and Sin waits at your door as a predator (with the desire to consume you). I want you to prevail against it, Cain. You must master it, so get out of your feelings, and do well."

What does it mean *to do well*?

Doing well means continuously striving toward excellence. As it relates to God, it means seeking to please Him, but our works alone are meaningless. They do not impress God, for He is perfect in every way, and everyone has fallen short of His glory. Therefore, the only way to do well in His sight is to walk with Him in obedience and faith **while** doing our best. Doing this will cause His favor to fall upon us. He will bless what we are doing for His glory and will smile upon us.

With that said, many wonder why God did not respect Cain's offering? I spent a lot of time contemplating this question myself. Did Cain offer mediocre fruit from the very ground God cursed after Adam and Eve had sinned; or was he was grumpy in giving to the LORD? Then again, perhaps Abel, through faith, offered a blood sacrifice, which was more in tune with the God's redemptive plan. The Bible tells us *almost all things are by the law purged with blood; and without shedding of blood, there is no remission of sin* (Hebrews 9:22). In my quest for answers, I asked fellow believers why God found Cain's offering to be unacceptable. The best answer I ever received was that Cain's sacrifice was out of place.

Several years ago, a brother in Christ whom I look up to explained to me that God wanted a blood sacrifice, but Cain did not walk by faith. It is written that "without faith, it is impossible to please God," according to Hebrews 11:6. Therefore, operating without faith, Cain offered a bloodless sacrifice which God supposedly did not want. My brother in Christ explained this to me, but I never truly accepted the answer he provided although I wanted to. I strongly believe that deep down, everyone recognizes the fullness of truth even if they proceed to subvert or deny it.

It so happened that many years later (as I was finishing this book), the Holy Spirit revealed the answer. If we know anything about God, it is that He loves a cheerful giver (2 Corinthians 9:6-7). He is also the same throughout time and never changes (c.f. Numbers 23:19, Hebrews 13:8, James 1:17). In the olden days, God accepted both blood offerings and those of fruit and grain. If all who offered fruit and grain did so in vain, He would have made it abundantly clear, but we know these offerings were acceptable. So, how do we harmonize this fact, and God's displeasure with Cain's offering?

Increasing our scriptural understanding often involves solving biblical riddles through informed, cross-referenced deduction. With help from the Holy Spirit, we can do this accurately! The Bible could have been ten times longer, but under divine inspiration, its writers conveyed incredible detail with superbly efficient composition. They initially wrote its manuscripts in a language whose very letters can represent entire words and notions! Those very letters comprise the words, which then convey God's message with deep individual and holistic importance! Additionally, we can take ideas from one section to then fill in blanks in others.

...all that to say this:

Although the reason God rejected Cain's offering is not specified in the book of Genesis, we can infer with a high degree of certainty that Cain did not offer his best fruit, and or He did not offer them with a cheerful heart! You see, Abel had animals while Cain had crops. Therefore, if anyone knew how to kill an animal for food and sacrifice, it was Abel; and if anyone knew how to grow food from the ground, it was Cain. It was not the type of offering, but the quality of their offerings that made one acceptable over another. In Leviticus 22:20, the Israelites were taught "whatsoever has a blemish, [that] shall you not offer, for it shall not be _acceptable_ for you. "Cain may not have picked the worst fruit, but they likely were not the best. Again, it was not the type of offering that made one more acceptable, but the heart behind each one (and God knows the heart). We can, therefore, infer that Abel was careful to select his best animal without blemish and give cheerfully, while Cain likely chose any ol' fruit or was disinclined in his giving. Just as God will readily give His children good things, He only accepts the same from us. Cain did not present a good offering. Therefore, God rejected it.

God gives us things that amaze us. If we want to offer Him something acceptable, we cannot give him mediocre gifts or give reluctantly. We should all want to astonish Him. Children who draw stick-figure family portraits do not really *amaze* their parents. Let us be honest with ourselves; most parents are not thinking, "Wow, this is the next Michael Angelo or Mary Cassatt!" Instead, they recognize their children's intent to amaze them, and good parents, show their approval. They encourage their little artists and may even put the drawings on display. Most parents are not blown away by "the raw talent" of their stick-figure-artists. Instead, they appreciate the hearts of the children who did well in trying to please them. Likewise, even though we know we cannot *amaze* God, our hearts should be set on trying to do that!

Good is not good enough. A man who wants an attractive woman to notice him will not buy her a gumball to win her heart (unless she is crazy about gumballs). Instead, he will do his best to win her affection with something that shows he wants that relationship. He will do something to show his heart is really in it. Likewise, someone who wants to give another person a meaningful gift should not think, "well, any ol' gift will do." I am sure you get the point. With God, it is not much different. Just because we will not blow Him away does not mean we should not try our best to please Him. God delights in us when we seek Him and learn to delight in Him.

CHAPTER 3
God's Love vs. His Righteous Judgment

God gives us good things even when we do not deserve them. The greatest gift He gave us was His only begotten son Jesus who was the perfect sacrifice and offering for the sins of the world. In other words, the sacrifice was complete! It lacked nothing! Christ's blood, which He shed for us, will never lose its power to redeem us! Therefore, we never have to sacrifice another lamb, turtledove, or anything else to atone for our sins. Those who accept Christ will one day be able to stand before the mighty and perfect God—not because we are good people, we give to the poor, or meditate a lot, but because God made a way!

Jesus, among other awesome things, is called the "first-born of all creation." In a sense, He became like an offering of blemish-free "first-fruit." Therefore, He was more than just a bloody sacrifice. Christ took upon Himself the punishment we all deserve, died, and was resurrected in victory. Now, all who believe in Him and do His will, share in the hope, and promise of everlasting life since He has become our Savior.

While some scientists may be optimistic about someday manufacturing a cure for mortality, I assure you—everything God set in motion must first run its course before people start living forever in either glorified bodies or cursed ones. Eternal life, according to Biblical teachings, is not the same as our definition of immortality. In the grand scheme of things, everyone will be immortal, but not everyone will have eternal life. Only those who dwell in God's presence will live forever, while those facing eternal destruction (or "eternal death") will ironically be immortal. Can you imagine being immortal and living in hell? What a terrible fate it would be!

Do we not know God is consistent and unbiased? He does not make exceptions. Unlike human beings who can be unfair, God executes His judgment with perfect consistency. While one person can bribe another, the earth is the LORD's and the fullness thereof; no one can bribe the LORD! Only by accepting His grace and mercy, and following the teachings of Christ, do we stand our only chance of escaping His judgment. Hell is real. It is an eternal life-sentence to a dismal realm devoid of hope, love, or mercy. Hell is the one place utterly bereft of God.

Here is an illustration:

Hell is inconceivably hot! Its flames torment forever as they lick and burn the flesh of its occupants. No air conditioner could ever relieve anyone there. It is a hopeless life of eternal separation from God's presence and mercy. Furthermore, all citizens of hell will experience complete darkness (besides that which hellfire illuminates), and let us be clear, the most terrifying creatures lurk in darkness. Every burning body part pertaining to an inmate of hell will regenerate forever only to be consumed again by fire.

We live in a world where we each are appointed to die once physically. On earth, nobody can end his or her life by mere desire. If one even tried to commit self-murder by holding his breath, at best, the poor fool might pass out only to start breathing again in his unconscious state. While we live in God's grace (here on earth), each of us can hope for something better. In hell, however, there is no savior and certainly no way out. There are no second chances at redemption. There is no longer any need for patience, love, humility, forgiveness, and other virtues. Instead, those who were wicked can still be wicked. Those who were hateful can cling to hate as they burn. Those who were liars, thieves, adulterers, given to violence, cruelty, etcetera will have chosen their fate. God will not accept them in His perfect world, where their presence would threaten to re-infect society with sin and iniquity.

You see, while there is yet time, we experience suffering as a reminder of our fall. The Bible says in Romans 8:22, "all creation groans and travails together." Furthermore, Jesus promised in John 16:33 that 'in this world, we would have trouble,' but he urged us to 'take courage for He has overcome the world.' Though tragedy can bring sorrow and pain, God wants us to endure. He wants us to learn wisdom, grow in faith and courage, learn to hope, persevere, love, forgive, and so much more! Those are His ways. His Kingdom will not be defiled by sin and darkness. Therefore, we must learn now how to be good citizens of the Kingdom of God.

We were not created to live for ourselves, but to live lives that glorify the Most High God, and <u>He will</u> be glorified whether through our obedience or rebellion. Therefore, let us seek the mutually beneficial option whereby we can praise and exalt our maker, let Him love us the way He wants to, and choose to love Him back. Every day we open our eyes in this world, it is because of His faithfulness, mercy, and kindness. He does not want anyone to perish but for all to be saved. Nevertheless, He will not force Himself upon anyone. Therefore, each of us gets to choose our fate.

Would you believe that when we live lives that glorify God, we live free from fear, deception, worry, hopelessness, addiction, etcetera, and we have real joy? We do not need to get high or drunk. The joy and peace of God are the only drugs we need. They follow us wherever we go because the Holy Spirit starts residing within us from the very moment we choose Christ over our sinful nature. Would you also believe that God cares so much for us that He came to die in exchange for our souls? Romans 5:8 says, "God demonstrates His love toward us, in that while we were still sinners, Christ died for us." No one else did that!

Hell is real. It is a place of eternal torment; a place God does not want any of us to go. Instead, He has a marvelous future Kingdom for everyone who accepts His love and salvation. Still, hell is a present danger to anyone who lives in their sins and a guarantee for all who die having chosen evil over Christ.

God did not create hell for human beings. Instead, it was a place in which God intended to cast Satan and his followers. Our creator is not cruel. He does not want anyone to perish but for all to come to repentance (2 Peter 3:9). He desires all people to be saved and to come to the knowledge of the truth, and He is incredibly patient as He waits for each person to choose wisely and open their minds and hearts to Him.

Since no one else was perfect, or even "good enough," we needed God to rescue us through Jesus. *"For there is one God and one Mediator between God and men, the Man Christ Jesus, who gave Himself a ransom for all, to be testified in due time"* (1 Timothy 2:3-5). The LORD is incredibly patient and compassionate. He is also kind and merciful, and He wants us to live full lives. When we live well, we glorify God, and we also benefit because we come from Him. Let us never forget He made us all in His image! When we are kind to others, we do good to ourselves also. When we forgive, we help ourselves heal. When we are patient, we learn to handle stress and anxiety productively. When we love, we learn to share the best of ourselves with others, and when we love God, we experience His love that much more!

Learning to love God is like holding someone who was trying to embrace you for a long time only to realize that a hug works better when two people commit to it. Dishonoring God when we lie, steal, cheat, and hurt others, brings harm to ourselves and others. It may not always be immediate, but one day, we will all be compensated handsomely for how we lived our lives. Though the wages of sin is death, the gift of God is eternal life in Christ Jesus, our Lord

(Romans 6:23). He offers us a gift that only He can give, but the choice is ours. All those who hate God love death (Proverbs 8:36).

When people consider the judgements of God upon the proud and unrepentant, many wonder how God can be so cruel. Why would a loving God sentence anyone to eternal doom and gloom? Does He not truly love the world?

The Bible tells us that God so loved the world that more than 2,000 years ago, He gave us His only begotten son Jesus Christ to be its savior. Even our calendars bear record that Christ lived on earth. For instance, this book was published in September of the year 2020 A.D. (an acronym for "Anno Domini", the year of our Lord). Every year that passes by from the approximate time of His birth is another year we count forward in time. History cannot erase the fact that Christ walked the earth. He died once and was resurrected by the power of God so that those who trust in Him will not perish but have eternal life with Him.

Whether the world knows it or not, humanity lives to glorify God one way or another through our decisions. In life, we face countless options. Even by not choosing, we decide upon something and still choose our fate. We cannot stop living by holding our breath or controlling our heartbeats; nor can we determine how old we will be, for we know not what the future holds. We can only make choices which affect our future.

God is not cruel. On the other side of His love, it certainly looks like hate, but by using imagery, we can better understand the consistency of His love. The presence of God in our lives is like being in a home with a well-lit fireplace. Those inside this house take refuge from the brutal blasts of winter. They sit by the fire and feel its warmth while those separated from the heat feel the frost. Those who are inside the house are comforted while cold winds attack those who are outside. Now, imagine God's presence as an air-conditioned home in the middle of a sweltering summer. Those who are outside restlessly seek relief. They take off articles of clothing, pour water on themselves, and do what they can to survive out there. In the meantime, those inside have found comfort and rest.

God does not hate anyone, but those who find themselves outside of the walls of His salvation perceive His love as hate. They have separated themselves from Him by their ignorance, disobedience, and pride. At present, they do not see why they must repent to avoid His wrath. Instead, they view His growing anger, the strictness of His commands, and His unwavering standards as valid reasons to steer clear of Him and fail to realize that He has never been the problem! He has been patient, merciful, and kind while we have taken those qualities for granted. There will come a time when the doors to His house will be locked so that no lover of evil will ever be able to harm a lover of righteousness again. That is good news for those who have accepted Christ.

Many were lost in the world. They were bullies, thieves, murderers, liars, etcetera. They were victims and perpetrators of evil, but now they cannot stand iniquity and never want to be the same again. Christ has changed them, and it is not too late to join His side.

We have all sinned and fallen short of God's glory. At one point, all were workers of iniquity, but some have humbled themselves, and others will humble themselves and turn toward the living, loving God before His grace is no longer available. They will find that He is indeed a good God. The rest will gnash their teeth and curse at Him because <u>He</u> did not shake them enough to get their attention. When they almost died in their sins, or when they were nearly killed, <u>He</u> did not make the message clear enough. When they nearly overdosed, got a terrible disease, were fired from a job, became homeless, or saw their family falling apart, it was not clear enough they were destroying themselves. Instead, it was always <u>His</u> fault because, during their lives, they had not learned humility and accountability for their actions. Instead, they always sought someone to blame. Many of them may think they were the "good" people, and ultimately, they will perceive God to be at fault for everything when their failure to yield cost them salvation. Let those who will listen to this message hear me now; the problem with humanity is us! Let us take accountability for our sins and glorify Christ as the one who died so that we could be free from our sins.

Dear reader, death has been our penalty from the moment our God promised it. A corrupted being cannot be restored to perfection without death and renewal. Thus, the diseased bodies of this mortal world must be shed, and we must be given new life to dwell forever with our righteous king.

CHAPTER 4
Bloody Hands

It is said that God shed the blood of animals to clothe Adam and Eve (Genesis 3:21). He sacrificed the first animals and humankind learned how to make clothing. Back then, there were no polyester garments, faux leathers, socks, or canvas shoes. Instead, coverings were made from what was available, primarily animals. God could have easily made Adam and Eve some high fashion clothing like the ones which appeal to our modern tastes, but the first clothes were not designed to impress anyone. Instead, they were made as humble coverings for our first parents. Their shameful fall and the subsequent guilt brought with it a realization of their nakedness. Therefore, clothing would be a perpetual reminder of their sin.

As God shed blood to cover Adam and Eve, the atonement for sin came through blood sacrifices and offerings until one day, the LORD would send His only begotten Son to be the final and everlasting sacrifice for sin. Sadly, though God wants all people to come to repentance, not everyone will choose the abundant life and joy He offers.

The Bible says in Matthew 7:13, "Enter through the narrow gate. For wide is the gate and broad is the way that leads to destruction, and many enter through it."

THE WAGES OF SIN

Sin is ready to pounce on those who do not strive for excellence because they are complacent. Many are okay with allowing their sins to control them throughout any given week as long as they go to church on Sunday or do their "good deed" for the day. Others do not care about doing good deeds. They just go about their lives with middle fingers up at God, the world, even their families, and other people. The Bible predicted that the world would drift farther and farther away from the knowledge of God.

Romans Chapter 1 describes a world strikingly like the one in which we now live. It talks about people who have exchanged the truth of God for a lie and do not see fit to acknowledge God. As a result, they are given over to depraved minds, to do things which are not proper. Those same individuals become filled with all unrighteousness, wickedness, greed, and evil. They are envious, murderous, full of strife, deceit, and malice. Their malice leads them to gossip about others, slander them, and hate God. They become insolent, arrogant, boastful, and inventors of evil. Additionally, they are disobedient to their parents, lack understanding, are untrustworthy, unloving, and unmerciful. Worse still is that they know God's ordinance against those who practice such things (that they deserve death), yet they not only do these evil things with pleasure but also support those who do the same (Romans 1:28-32 paraphrased).

Cain was one of those. Soon after the LORD had spoken with him, Cain and his brother Abel conversed with each other. At some point, Cain became enraged, for he struck his brother and killed him!

Let us imagine the first historical homicide as it occurred. What was going through Cain's envious and murderous brain in that terrifying moment? Well, for one thing, it was sending the signals required for his body to act out violently. Its role in the assault had simply been to process the visuals (among billions of other computations that he was not even aware of)! It was making sense of the environment so that Cain could target his brother, orient himself, adjust his motion, and deliver the fatal blow with precision. Still, his brain (like ours) was just the hardware through which his soul connected to the physical world. It merely signaled his body to act according to the will of his mind (spirit-heart-brain/ "inner soul"). Remember, the brain alone does not decide. It only receives vast quantities of environmental info, processes them into a simplified format for the spirit to "read," transmits impulses to the body, and regulates processes within the body.

Cain contemplated the evil that he had known, entertained it, and now, Sin was upon him! At that very moment, he should have mastered it, but instead, he allowed it to control him! As God had implicitly forewarned, Cain became a slave to his anger, which had grown into hatred manifested through violence all because he had not sought to do well. So, there we have it, —the first documented murder in history explained—not from a psychiatric point of view, but—from a **soul science** point of view.

Psychiatrists often diagnose murderers as either sociopaths or psychopaths. They study the brains of those with violent urges and notice abnormal activities consistent with people said to have personality disorders. As a result, they conclude that murderers have a certain "kind of brain." That is false. Recall from the first chapter that the mind is the spirit working in tandem with the brain. The brain's activity is not only influenced by injury and chemical imbalances, but by the spirit which interfaces with it. Therefore, if a violent spirit interacts with a healthy brain, the activity of the brain *will undoubtedly* appear to be consistent with that of a brute. It is merely displaying the symptoms of an internal problem as when a virus has infected a computer.

When a digital virus attacks a computer, it results in abnormal activity. The machine itself may not be physically damaged, but something has hijacked it. Likewise, spirit beings can interact with flesh and even usurp bodily control of willing or weak hosts. This "hijacking" has happened to countless people and animals who were said to be "demon-possessed." The errors in Psychiatric knowledge are the result of the same cause of blunder in other branches of science, ignorance of God and His truths.

Secular psychiatrists evaluate abnormal people by examining their brains. Little do they know that God did not create us as beings of pure flesh. Instead, we are hybrids of flesh and spirit. Therefore, analyzing the CPU, we call the human brain is futile unless we understand that brain activity does not encapsulate most of our being. Furthermore, it is not even the place in which thoughts originate! It is, however, a place in which ideas take more material forms to then be manifested through visible actions (once we commit to our will to act). The brain manages and regulates most biological functions to some extent while also interpreting sensory inputs (from the environment) and sensory outputs (from the spirit) to the body. An excellent example of how the brain merely processes incoming and outgoing information is the average stroke survivor.

Stroke patients often lose functionality in regions of their brains, yet their identities, memories, and personalities remain the same. Their brains never controlled who they were, although, through their body-brain connections, they were able to visibly demonstrate their character through actions.

Under normal circumstances, few people can see the spirit of one's consciousness. Yet we can quickly understand someone's personality through their actions which are visible manifestations of their invisible urges. For instance, one can anyone tell if someone is impatient through body language (perhaps the impatient individual paces back and forth, taps his or her feet), or says something like "hurry up!", "any day now!" etcetera. How can one tell that another is a murderer? Simple, murderers display their propensity and readiness to kill! Remember, the brain controls **how** we interact with the world and manifest our will through the action of our bodies. It is not the source of our personality, but it is the spirit-to-body interface that enables us (primarily spirit beings) to function within a physical plane of existence.

Damage to a part of the brain does not affect personality. Such injury only affects areas of the body its "wires" connect to.

If we go back to the illustration of stroke patients, we have gained a better understanding of how those personally injured by a stroke often lose mobility and experience impaired speech. The brain is only hardware through which the spirit "drives" the body. Stroke patients generally do not turn into different people. If ever they do not seem like themselves, they likely miss the abilities they have lost. We cannot correctly understand and appreciate the brain without acknowledging **we are spiritual beings first and foremost**!

Cain was not born with a sociopathic brain, but he was born into sin as all humans are. He allowed his sinful thoughts and desires to control his actions until he killed his brother. After the incident, God visited Cain and asked where his brother was, though God already knew. It was reminiscent of the way the LORD had visited Adam and Eve after their eyes had been "opened" through their disobedience. God sought them out after they made their choice. Was it a coincidence that He was now visiting Cain? Not a chance! Was God to blame for either of the incidents? No! The LORD does, however, seem to remove himself from our decision-making process once he has given us the warnings and 'tools' needed to conquer sin if we so *choose*. As a respecter of our free will, He sees to it that He does not interfere with our choices unless we ask Him to be the Lord of our lives! He very much respects the free agency He gave us even if we use it to do wrong.

And the LORD said unto Cain, "Where is Abel thy brother?" And Cain said, "I know not: Am I my brother's keeper?" - Genesis 4:9

At once, God revealed to Cain what he had already known.

"And He said, "What have you done? "The voice of your brother's blood cries unto me from the ground." - Genesis 4:10

Cain's punishment (for murdering his brother) was severe. He became the first human whom the LORD explicitly cursed.

*"And now you are **cursed** from the earth, which has opened her mouth to receive your brother's blood from your hand; When you till the ground, it shall not henceforth yield unto you her strength; a fugitive and a vagabond shall you be in the earth." -Genesis 4:11 & 12*

Cain had not imagined the consequences of his actions before performing them. He allowed his wicked thoughts toward his brother to take over him, and now his misdeed and the result of it were made clear to him.

"Behold, you have driven me out this day from the face of the earth; and from your face shall I be hidden; and I shall be a fugitive and a wanderer in the earth; and it shall come to pass, that anyone that finds me shall slay me." -Genesis 4:14

The LORD could have struck Cain down instantly after he murdered his brother, if not for the murder itself, for his attitude when he had cynically replied, "Am I my brother's keeper?" Again, however, the LORD was merciful even when we could probably agree that Cain did not deserve this mercy. When Cain admitted his fear of being murdered himself, the Lord said to him:

"Therefore, whoever slays Cain, vengeance shall be taken on him sevenfold. And the LORD set a mark upon Cain, lest any finding him should kill him."

Thus, Cain had the protection of the LORD through the mark that signified his curse. The Bible states that some time afterward, Cain "found a wife" and "multiplied." It does not say precisely where Cain found his wife, but:

"Adam called his wife's name Eve; because she was the <u>mother of all living</u>." - Genesis 3:20

Therefore, in an age before incest became forbidden, we can infer that Cain married one of his sisters. Bear in mind, his parents continued to be "fruitful," as the LORD had instructed. By the time of her death, Eve had conceived and delivered more children into the world than most women in all known history! Remember, the LORD had promised her that He would greatly multiply her sorrow **and** her conception (Gen 3:16). The famous historian Josephus wrote in "Antiquities of the Jews, Book 1: "The number of Adam's children, as says the old tradition, was 33 sons and 23 daughters." That was written in Chapter 2, Paragraph 2, Endnote 8 of the book.

While 56 children are quite copious, Adam and Eve lived over 900 years without contraceptive technology! They could have had many more progeny. Our current Bibles (consisting of all the manuscripts found by the 5th century A.D.) do not include the exact amount of offspring they had. Furthermore, that information is not critical, although it would have been nice to have.

So, Cain found a wife in his immediate family and although some might be disgusted by this, we need to understand that incest was abolished first among God's followers and for a specific reason. For centuries, incest has been frowned upon and even forbidden, but we forget that it was not always so. Incest was historically practiced by "elite" members of society (royal families, etc.) to keep bloodlines "pure," even after God made it forbidden.

Incest, according to modern knowledge, is notorious for its tendency to result in genetic defects. Still, it was not until human beings began to study genetics that they realized what God had already known! Humankind was once more vigorous in the time of Adam and Eve, and their genes were once perfect. However, when corruption entered the world, human genes began to deteriorate. As a result, God forbade it first among the ancient Israelites before the world followed suit. Incest did not become taboo because siblings are reproductively incompatible. Furthermore, human beings do not just "naturally" find it unappealing. Remember that even royal families historically preserved their bloodlines through incestuous marriages long after Biblical times. Moreover, it has been discovered that unusually strong sexual attraction tends to occur between siblings, half siblings, and cousins who did not know each other as children, but meet for the first time as adults. Though these events are often the unintended consequence of short-sighted parental decisions, they are nonetheless real.

At any rate, God understood that the genetic vigor of His creation would decline when Adam and Eve sinned. He knew that closeness in genetic proximity would begin to cause problems as genes became less and less perfect. Indeed, this degradation has continued to our present day. Allergies are increasing, and the genetic vigor and nutritional value of plants are decreasing. Bee populations are affected by an onslaught of diseases that threaten their very existence, Tasmanian devils have experienced a strange facial tumor, and the list goes on. God decided—based on his advanced knowledge of genetics and other factors that incest had to end. In the book of Leviticus, thousands of years before modern man *learned* to be disgusted by it, God ended it among the Israelites. Nowadays, although we still marry relatives (since **all** human beings are related), our partners are usually distant relatives of the human kind.

CHAPTER 5
Evil Reign of the god-Kings

Despite Adam and Eve's sorrow over Abel's death, they were hopeful of God's promise to rescue and restore humanity. Before God cast them out of the garden, He promised He would avenge and restore them (c.f. Genesis 3:15). Following their creator's instructions, Adam and Eve multiplied with sons and daughters. Among them, they had a son named Seth. He and his children were said to be righteous, and their children after them. Even so, the worsening condition of the earth grieved the LORD.

To make matters worse, the Bible states:

"It came to pass, when men began to multiply on the face of the earth, and daughters were born unto them, that the sons of God saw the daughters of men that they were fair; and they took them wives of all which they chose." -Gen 6:1-2

Then, the Bible describes the offspring of this unsanctified union of angelic and human beings, where it states:

"There were giants in the earth in those days; and also after that, when the sons of God came in unto the daughters of men, and they bore children to them, the same became mighty men which were of old, men of renown." -Genesis 6:4

Genesis 6:4 indicates rebel angels mated with the "daughters of men" to produce a superhuman race of giants called the "Nephilim." These were abominations to God and were the product of sin and rebellion. The defilement of humans and angels, as well as the subsequent rise of the Nephilim, resulted in more corruption and violence on the earth.

And the LORD said, "My spirit shall not always strive with man, for that he also is flesh: yet his days shall be a hundred and twenty years." - Genesis 6: 3

Some Bible commentators insist Genesis 6 verses 1-4, refers to a union between the sons of Seth (Adam's "good" line hence "the sons of God") and the daughters of Cain (Adam's sinful and wicked descendants). The scriptures, however, do not say this. Instead, they clearly refer to angels, their giant offspring, and the "demigods" of the ancient world. In fact, we have even unearthed a remarkable amount of evidence supporting the existence of a race of superhuman giants!

We can only speculate on how purely spiritual entities mated with human beings. In the first chapter of this book, we established that spirits *could* interact with flesh. We deduced this from the very fact that **human beings are spirits living in human flesh**. The constant interaction of energies influences our perception of physical reality. Still, everything consists of a spiritual component, and the Bible tells us that the things we see came from that which we cannot see. For instance, atoms can fill an area that is perceived to be empty, and yet they can also occupy other spaces in forms that we clearly identify as tangible and visible matter (or objects). Individual atoms have no real connection to other particles beyond their interacting fields of energy. Therefore, the consistency of a substance (whether it's hard, soft, permeable, liquid, vaporous, etc.) has everything to do with its energy fields. That is the purported explanation for our world's tangibility. Bearing this in mind, consider how our immaterial spirits interface with our physical brains, which then enable our bodies to interact with our world. It is a phenomenon we do not fully understand, but it is a fact. Likewise, the "sons of God" (spoken of in Genesis 6) were spiritual entities who decided to intermingle with human women. They succeeded because spirits **can** interact with flesh.

There is much debate as to whether spirit beings can have sex. Some believe they can (research **incubus** and **succubus** spirits). The very act of "sex" is often speculated to have a "spiritual" component. Many believe the spirits of two individuals unite and imprint upon each other during sexual intercourse. That is why a breakup tends to be more painful after both partners have formed a "soul tie." The physical act called "sex" has consequences, for it is an outward display of an invisible spiritual entanglement.

Even so, a spiritual entanglement theory perhaps overcomplicates how fallen angels were able to mate with humans. God created everything to mate with (and produce *after*) *its kind*. Therefore, spirits should not be able to reproduce with flesh. Only flesh can reproduce with its kind. Nevertheless, spirits **can** interact with flesh. You are a living demonstration of this notion by the very control you (as a being of spiritual essence) have over the mech suit you call your body. So how do we harmonize the two ideas that living beings can only reproduce after their kind and yet invisible spirits can interact with flesh?

The first step perhaps may be to define and understand spiritual possession. Possession is ownership. The spirit in each of our bodies owns and controls our bodies while God permits us to live in this world. There are, however, ways for other spirits to enter our bodies, influence us, and even take absolute control of us! The spirit of God, for instance, has come upon Biblical figures such as Othniel (in Judges 3:10) and Samson (in Judges chapter 14 verses 5-6 and verse 19 as well as Judges chapter 15 verses 14-15) to endow them with supernatural strength, will, courage, wisdom, speed, and other powers. Yes, God's Holy Spirit has, at times, possessed people who needed His help. But God's spirit is not the only one that can enter people to possess them (and spiritually overpower them).

Many have heard of demonic possession. Those possessed by a demon or demons may not immediately recognize their influence. They may reflect upon their unjustified emotional outbursts, behaviors, and or decisions, but often they only understand the magnitude of the situation once the demonic entities have established full operational control and turned them into backseat passengers (so to speak).

In the case of the **Nephilim** (the children of the fallen angels), is it possible for them to have hacked reproduction through spirit possession? After all, if the Satan could have usurped the body of a serpent (as explained in "The Serpent's Lie," the prequel to this book), then fallen angels could have used men's bodies for their pleasures while gaining the ability to impregnate women. Recall the following fundament—*spirit animates flesh.*

The human body consists of trillions of cells which all interact as part of **one** unit. That means that cellular activity began when God breathed the Spirit of Life into all His creatures. A spirit that God sends into a lifeless body can cause even the smallest functional units within it to come to life. In contrast, a body whose spirit has departed immediately dies right down to its last cell.

Imagine a sperm cell animated by the spirit of a man. Now imagine that same cell enhanced by the spirit of a powerful foreign entity who cohabits the man's body. Such an enhanced cell could produce enhanced offspring if the foreign spirit used the host to reproduce. If this powerful entity were a fallen angel, for instance, one could then say that the "sons of God" fathered the enhanced beings.

Victims of spirit possession can summon supernatural strength, the type of power which requires several people to overcome. That is because demons are powerful spirits. As you recall, spirits are the essence of life, and therefore have the power to energize every cell in their hosts. Thus, a powerful spirit can increase the strength of the body it influences as the spirit of God strengthened Samson whenever it came upon him.

How does strength manifest itself in the appearance of living creatures? Let us examine humans, more specifically. Usually, stronger people are taller and have higher skeletal and muscular density than weaker individuals. We can only imagine how much more powerful angelic beings are than humans. Based on Biblical descriptions of angelic power, we can logically conclude that the offspring of a fallen one could grow supernaturally large. We call it flexing when we flaunt strength by contracting our muscles. It is nonverbal display, effective at helping us estimate the strength of others. So, if a giant flexed in our presence, we could likewise surmise its terrifying power.

Another way an angel may have been able to mate with a human being is by taking on the form of one. Angels have assumed the appearance of men in the Bible, perhaps most notably the two who rescued Lot and his family from the destruction of Sodom and Gomorrah. They looked human enough that the rowdiest among the homosexual men of Sodom lusted after them with an intent to rape them, and they did try.

In living things, genotype expression determines the physical appearance. A genotype is an entire collection of genes that constitute an organism. This collection of genes contains information that contributes to eye color, complexion, potential height, etc. Genes have coded instructions that cells use to build the bodies of living organisms and execute bodily functions. If angels contain information systems within their spiritual bodies and they assume the form of human beings, it may be that their own biological information codes can approximate those of a human to express the physical appearance they wish to assume.

We currently do not have all the answers, but one way or another, many former angels tampered with God's world to bring about abominations. In the meantime, human beings were proving themselves to be quite wicked and sinful. The LORD responded by saying that His spirit would not always strive with man and that he would only give humanity a hundred and twenty years to live.

Many believers and scholars interpret God's promise as a reduction of man's lifespan. We would go from living several centuries to living a maximum average of 120 years. Adam had lived to be 930 years old! His son Seth lived 912 years, and it was not uncommon for the first generations of humans to live that long. God has since curtailed our lifespans.

Few people ever see past their 120th birthday. It is my firm belief that **IF** this is the meaning of Genesis 6:3, then the ***average*** lifespan will **<u>never</u>** exceed 120 years of age (naturally) until after the second coming of the LORD. The LORD, Creator of all things, spoke it. Therefore, His will is final.

Another interpretation of the promise in Gen 6:3 is that God was giving a grace period. Perhaps the grace period exegesis coincided with the "120-year average lifespan limit" in a clever double entendre by God, who sometimes speaks polysemically.

In the age of giants, humankind indulged in all manner of sin and immorality. Violence filled the earth. There was, however, one man named Noah, who found favor in God's sight. After 120 years had elapsed, only he and his family were spared. They trusted the LORD and obeyed His commands. Therefore, God resolved to save Noah and his family. As for the rest of the world, God declared destruction, for they had erased and redrawn moral boundaries that He had established (just as society continues to do even today).

Humanity sinned with reckless abandon. The pre-flood era became an age where "anything goes," much like our modern world. Noah's contemporaries got drunk, were merry, and indulged in all the sensual fun they craved.

And the LORD said, I will destroy man whom I have created from the face of the earth; both man, and beast, and the creeping thing, and the fowls of the air; for it repenteth me that I have made them. -Gen 6: 7

And God said unto Noah, "The end of all flesh is come before me; for the earth is filled with violence through them; and, behold, I will destroy them with the earth." - Gen 6:13

And, behold, I, even I, do bring a flood of waters upon the earth, to destroy all flesh, in which is the breath of life, from under heaven; and everything that is in the earth shall die. But with you will I establish my covenant; and you shall come into the ark, you, and your sons, and your wife, and your sons' wives with you. -Gen 6:17-18

Of fowls after their kind, and of cattle after their kind, of every creeping thing of the earth after its kind, two of every sort shall come unto you, to keep them alive. -Gen 6:20

For yet seven days, and I will cause it to rain upon the earth forty days and forty nights; and every living thing that I have made will I destroy from off the face of the earth. -Gen 7:4

Today, many consider ancient giants and the Great flood to have been myths as if the whole world had experienced powerful hallucination. There are indeed accounts of giants and a worldwide flood from a myriad of countries around the world. There is also much evidence to corroborate both. For instance, archaeologists have found fossils of marine animals in the mountains of every continent! This evidence is consistent with a worldwide flood. Likewise, there is compelling evidence of giants. Many of their fossils have also been found all around the world, especially between the 1800s and the 21st century! Many ancient artworks and historical records further support their existence.

Some of the earliest records known to man capture the existence of the famous giants thought by most to be merely fictional. Many old writing systems, such as the hieroglyphs of ancient Egypt, were photographic, depicting giants as rulers who towered over ordinary human beings and even sizable animals. Ancient sculptures also captured the image, likeness, and supernatural proportions of their "god-kings" and "demigod-heroes." Additionally, sources such as the Sumerian "legend" of Gilgamesh and Greek "mythology," among others around the world, retell the sagas of giants and even the Great flood.

If ancient scrolls kept record of ancient events and modern history purposefully overlooks them for whatever excuse it provides, our recent tampering should not invalidate the original accounts. If my grandfather journaled his entire life, his journals would still recount his times better than the collective speculation or "intelligent guessing" of all my contemporaries combined!

Cultures from all over the world (even those which at the time had developed independently) knew of the giants and recorded them in writing. Excluding fossil evidence, which is compelling enough on its own, there are too many similarities in the folklore about giants for us to ignore. For example, they often warred with the gods (e.g., Titans vs. Olympian gods, Nephilim vs. God). They were also described as violent, even cannibalistic, and often associated with the "demigod" sect.

In those days, it is believed, based on ancient records, that heavenly beings periodically visited human civilizations. They were known to possess incredible knowledge and even abilities, which include traveling from place to place with unparalleled speed! That could potentially explain how so many megalithic structures separated by great distances, oceans, hostile terrains, etc. resemble one another. For example, while ancient Egyptians had pyramids dedicated to "pharaohs" (god-kings), Aztec and Mayan civilizations living several thousand miles away had pyramidal ziggurats for their gods and kings. There is a pyramidal edifice in Cambodia, called the "Prang Temple," which ancient Cambodians dedicated to a "god-king." Back then, the world lacked the technology needed to travel across continents separated by vast oceans neither could they transmit information. Therefore, such commonalities are found from an era long before explorers and colonizers like Columbus and Magellan even "discovered" lands they would have considered "New" Worlds.

There are too many shared elements in folklore, architecture, and religious practices of the ancient pre-internet, pre-cell phone, and pre-worldwide-communication era to overlook or consider as mere coincidence. Additionally, the concepts of half-human half-divine beings such as giants, demi-gods, or god-kings were so prevalent that they could not have arisen from thin air! Suggesting a coincidence would either be an act of denial or a deliberate attempt to deceive. Ancient Egyptians and Cambodians were not the only cultures to believe in demigods. Many other cultures believed that they had been visited by deities who dwelt among them and mated with human beings. According to our understanding of the Bible, there are no other deities. Therefore, they were, indeed, imposters. After all, Yahweh, the LORD God Almighty is the only God and creator of the world.

CHAPTER 6
Gods of the Ancient World

To a human being, a god is a superior entity that one worships and or fears for having power over nature, fortune, and destiny. To one who lacks knowledge of our supreme and unique God, angelic beings might fall under that category, for they ***are*** indeed mighty. Therefore, it is not surprising that the appearance of angels has evoked awe and fear throughout ancient history. The phrase "Do not be afraid" often followed angelic apparitions recorded in the Bible. They would often say that before delivering divine messages because, according to their Biblical descriptions, angels are terrifyingly glorious.

Believers of the Biblical God of "gods," often teach that He is the only god. It makes sense that all authority ultimately converges into a singularity. If powerful figures divested their power and centrality of command were lost, the result would be unregulated autonomy (which would sooner or later become chaos). Imagine a world without government, or households without good parents (who set rules and boundaries). Imagine companies devoid of centralized leadership. Visualize a world where everyone did as they pleased. It would be turbulent! Therefore, only fools believe there is no God and even wish for it to be true.

Throughout history, the world has experienced conflicts of interest, which began first as personal or individual ones. Most of us can recall at least one point in our lives when we wanted to do the right thing, but the wrong thing to do felt easier or more gratifying in the moment. That was an internal conflict of interest. We "sinned" by knowingly choosing wrong even if we were able to 'rationalize' our misdeed and make excuses. Internal conflicts of interests develop into interpersonal ones when we do not control them, and then societal ones. By now, in efforts to evade accountability and guilt, the world has exchanged the truth of God for a lie, and it glorifies the creature above the Creator as the bible foretold in the book of Romans Chapter one.

The God who made everything cannot be made just as one who built a house had to exist before the house he built. Yahweh, our creator, has no origin. The gods of myths and legends, on the other hand, have beginnings. In most of the more popular myths, they were the offspring of male sky gods and female earth goddesses (as in Greek mythology, which begins with the sky god "Uranus" and the earth goddess "Gaia").

Modern scientists unanimously agree that the formation of the cosmos preceded the creation of the earth, but even the universe is known to have an origin. Therefore, Uranus, the mythological sky-god, for instance cannot be the creator of everything. We understand that makers of things precede the things they make. The maker of the cell phone was born before the cellphone existed, so too were the makers of the first television, airplane, car, and everything else that has ever been made. The one being who lived before all others is the very one who created all others.

The fact of this matter is evident when we look it right in the eyes. God created heaven, earth, and everything in them, and because most people do not want to deal with the truth, they would rather say the Universe came to be by itself, and then it made us. The real God of Creation could not have been created. He must always have existed, for if He made space, time, and matter, He had to precede them all, including the false gods of the world. Those false gods are the powerful fallen beings and their offspring, which the ancient world regarded as deities. They were the very same who fathered the Nephilim of biblical accounts, also known as giants in various world myths, such as those of the Norse people, and Titans of the Greek and Roman lore. No "gods" existed before Yahweh. He is the one true and living deity.

When we spell God (as in the one true God), we capitalize the "G" to signify His supremacy over all others; but why is He called the God of gods if there are no other gods? Furthermore, why did He say, "You shall have no other gods before me" in Deuteronomy 5:7? Would that not be akin to me telling you that you should read no other books besides mine? The very nature of such a command would imply that other books exist. Likewise, the LORD implies that there are indeed other gods—well, sort of.

Anything one worships *becomes* a "god"—**to the worshipper**, even if it is a lifeless idol. That is why God said, "Thou shalt have no other gods before me," yet also said, "I am the LORD, and there is none else, there is no God beside me" (Isaiah 45:5). We must harmonize these seemingly contradictory statements to understand the truth.

God said that we should not place any "gods" before Him, for He is the only true God who is worthy of our praise. Nothing else is worthy —not objects, nor animals, nor people! Our Heavenly Father is the single true and **living** deity among inanimate idols, frauds, and distractions. However, because people tend to deify things when they do not know God, or feel like He has forsaken them, does not exist, or should not be worshipped, He commanded us not to have any other gods before him; for the things we worship **are** gods (to us) even if they are not at all divine.

For though there be those called gods, whether in heaven or in earth, (as there be gods many, and lords many,)
But to us there is but one God, the Father, of whom are all things, and we in him; and one Lord Jesus Christ, by whom are all things, and we by him. -1 Cor 8: 5-6

As you already know, angels are extravagantly powerful beings. Relative to a human, they are powerful enough to be perceived as deities. Their powers, however, came from the source of all—the Creator of the heavens, the earth, and all their inhabitants—Yahweh, the LORD, our omnipotent God! When rebel angels chose human wives on earth, they stayed among human civilizations just long enough for false religions to arise in their honor. Ancient stories that we now consider to be mythical or legendary have originated from their involvement in human affairs.

It is not difficult to see why our ancient ancestors worshiped those advanced beings clothed in glory. Nevertheless, it angered God, for He had not created them to be praised. The birth of human-angel hybrids (or "demigods") further angered the LORD. Earth was a separate realm created for humanity's dominion (as we were created after the likeness of God). Though God knew beforehand that society would descend into darkness, when it happened, it broke his heart that He had created human beings on earth (c.f. Genesis 6:6). Still, however, God is so concerned with humankind's state of being and His redemptive plan for the world that throughout history, He has shown us grace. Remember that since the fall of man, He's been working to restore a relationship with us.

CHAPTER 7
Two of Every Kind

The story of the flood has been retold all around the world with few changes. There is an apparent reason for such a congruity—it happened! Subsequently, it spread by oral, and then written tradition. In this chapter, we will explore the Biblical narrative and compare it to similar stories.

The LORD God said unto Noah, "The end of all flesh has come before Me; for the earth is filled with violence through them; and, behold, I will destroy them with the earth." -Gen 6:13

"And, behold, I, even I, do bring a flood of waters upon the earth, to destroy all flesh, wherein is the breath of life, from under heaven; and everything that is in the earth shall die.
But with thee will I establish my covenant; and thou shalt come into the ark, thou, and thy sons, and thy wife, and thy sons' wives with thee." - Gen 6:17-18

God made sure to prepare Noah for what was to come. He told Noah to build an ark that would keep him and his family safe. The LORD also commanded Noah to bring pairs of each kind of animal (one male and one female) aboard the ark to preserve their kinds. Every other human being and every other animal upon the face of the earth would be wiped out of existence.

The Biblical flood is one of the most misunderstood accounts. Many wonder how Noah was able to cram all the Earth's animals into one ark. After all, there are so many different types of animals that exist today. Even that massive ark was not large enough to make such a feat possible! However, when God instructed Noah to bring two of every <u>kind</u> of animal into the ark, somehow, Noah was able to do it. Before we discuss how he accomplished such a monumental task, I would like to make a few things clear.

Reading the Bible requires a certain state of mind. People cannot understand its depth nor its truth if they are not ready to let go of secular mindsets and conditioned ways of thinking. We should not impose our current, limited worldview upon our ancient ancestors. Life was not the same for them as it is for us. Our experience is influenced by modern amenities such as technology, institutions such as the government, ideologies such as which political affiliation we should lean toward, moral perceptions, etc.

Although it seems evident that Biblical times were different, than our present day, we often find it difficult to imagine the world as it was from the eyes of our ancestors. We should make a conscious effort to willfully let go of what we know (or think we know) about the nature of reality. Often, we base it off of our modern-day lifestyles.

When I wrote this book, the world population consisted of approximately 7.6 billion human souls! In our world today, there are many different ethnicities. In biblical times, however, the world consisted of *far* fewer people and nations!

According to ecology.com, in the year 1 AD, there were between 170 and 400 million people in the world! The lower estimate is almost half of the current population of the United States alone, while the higher estimate is nearly a quarter of the current Chinese population. In other words, there were much, much fewer nations back then.

All the different peoples of the world, in all their shades, descended from the Father and Mother of human**kind**, Adam and Eve. The same is true for most animals. They descended from two original ancestral pairs. Recall that God had created everything to reproduce after its **kind**. For the next chapter, it will be crucial to understand what a "kind" is, primarily since we casually use the term whenever we speak of "man*kind*". Rarely do we contemplate the origin of that term.

A jaguar, leopard, and black panther are all the same kind (or category of wild cat). Did you know that? Although biological taxonomy categorizes jaguars and leopards as different species under the same genus, they are as much the same kind of cat as a person born in China is to a person born in India. Even if their coloration varies (as human pigmentation also does), they can all mate with each other and reproduce. Lions, tigers, jaguars, leopards, and panthers are all reproductively compatible! They are of the same kind just as all people (even from different ethnic backgrounds) are part of the human (Adamic) kind (or type).

MAV JR.

CHAPTER 8
The Great Delusion

Many people profess themselves to be wise. They can be quite scathing when someone questions their worldviews. Those who reject the one true God continue to search elsewhere for their origins and purposes. Not only have they become blind to the truth, —they have also led others into error and their pride loathes correction.

In the 1970s, scientists discovered a fossilized hominid which they called "Lucy." They claimed it was one of the missing links between man and ape, but it was not a missing link at all. By now, Lucy has been debunked not only by virtually **all** creationist scientists but also most evolutionary ones.

When faced with the truth of God and "junk science," many choose the junk. They use evidence that easily supports creation to persuade others there is no God. Meanwhile, their search for missing links continues. It is a wild goose chase because, quite frankly, **they do not exist** (for any animal)! If we can find dinosaur fossils from an era allegedly long before humankind, there is no reason we cannot find much more recent fossils to link us to apes. We cannot even find a single shred of fossil evidence showing an animal transitioning into a new kind of creature!

We have found fossils of animals that were in the process of consuming smaller prey moments before they were fossilized. This strongly indicates earth's "gradual" sedimentary processes did not bury them! I am not proposing that sedimentation does not occur at all, but we have observed that every dead animal decomposes too quickly to be preserved for millions of years by such slow burial processes as sedimentation. It takes particular sets of circumstances (such as freezing in ice, mummification, or fossilization by earth or amber) for something as readily biodegradable as a corpse to be preserved for months, let alone thousands of years. That means most of our current fossil evidence must have resulted from catastrophes like Noah's flood. Yet the secular mind is hard to convince, and it is not hard to see why.

As a child, I spent more time being "raised" by educators in schools than my parents. From 8 a.m. to 3 p.m. every school day, my young mind was being shaped by an educational system designed to perpetuate a secular worldview. My parents were often unavailable until after 5 p.m. We then spent two to three meaningful hours together in the evening before it was bedtime, and then I rinsed and repeated. Extended quality time happened during the weekends if Saturday morning cartoons and other television *programs* did not take their place. During my college years, I was even more influenced by professors. It was challenging to find freedom from the mental prison that the academic world had built around my mind to separate me from God. Since the universe was so vast, I was taught that human beings were insignificant.

The school system forced the acceptance of a big bang upon me with little room for questioning. Current educational tactics teach people (from youth) how to question things within a framework of what is deemed academically acceptable or appropriate. In fact, most teachers who profess the belief of a Godless origin would frown upon a student who dared to point out that all evidence more accurately supports the Biblical account of creation. That is quite unfortunate, especially since no rational mind ever concluded that a functional system, structure, or contraption could have ever formed itself, until Darwin popularized such an absurd notion. It was clear to the world that an intelligent creator or pagan creators designed everything around us.

In a world where a great delusion prevails like a mass-produced item, there must be a source responsible for perpetuating it. Schools take advantage of the fertile "soil" in the minds of children, implanting ideas into their susceptible heads. Children, in turn, become seeds that someday replant themselves into society and shape its destiny. As many companies in the food industry have removed vital nutrients from the foods they sell, schools (in like manner) have "processed" their lessons and removed the most important foundations of truth.

Young minds are being mentally fed with part substance, part fluff. Even as nutrient-deficient food will fill one's stomach, false knowledge will fill the minds of the young pupils taught they have no creator. As junk food must appear nutritional and digestible enough for someone to eat it, false knowledge must have some substance to it, otherwise no one would believe it! Pseudoscientists may sound insightful, speculating about the events that led to our existence. They may seem to have a lot of answers, but they mislead.

Most people at one point or another have wondered about humanity's origins. They came hungry (intellectually), seeking to be fed with truth, and instead, they got filler food that never truly satisfied them. Sure, they were intellectually challenged by having to memorize pseudoscientific lies, but their spiritual growth was denied.

I think about the number of students who enter the academic world, then get pumped out into the so-called "real world." After bidding farewell to Academia, countless people get jobs and find new routines. Most adults having been molded by school systems join the increasingly poor workforce, advancing someone else's goals and agendas while denying their own purposes, dreams, talents, and spiritual growth. Their new routines continue to keep them so preoccupied they have little time to contemplate much else.

I think about the connection between the decline of God-fearing people (those who follow God's laws, not just calling themselves "Christians" or "Jews", but trying to live in deed and by deed as followers of Christ) and the increase in civil unrest, fear, worry, hate…etc. There is most assuredly a correlation between them.

I consider the corruption of young, innocent, and vulnerable minds from youth and the continued programming through television, media, books, etc. We are taught that we are not special. Some might wake up from this lie, not realizing the deception is more layered and profound than they could have imagined. Thus, they wake from one dream only to find themselves in another; and still, they sleep (spiritually).

Some people start searching for God within themselves through inner reflection, yogic meditation, etc. Deep down, they are partially right in seeing divinity within themselves (since God made us in His likeness), yet they are far from the truth. They exalt themselves, not realizing they are not God and that "self, self, self" is the way of our current world. God wants us to remain in the truth by following Him first, putting others second, and placing ourselves last. It is counterintuitive, especially considering that not everyone is friendly, courteous, or appreciative; but can you imagine if the world operated like this? It would be more like God's perfect Kingdom! Instead, most look out for themselves and their interests.

A world that does not seek God cannot see His love. It does not realize how incredibly mindful He is of each person. It chooses to believe it resulted from a cosmic accident. Since the imaginations of developing minds are more susceptible, they can be taught that "The Universe" or "Nature" occasionally makes mistakes. Resultantly, children start thinking, "maybe Mother Nature intended for me to be a boy, but made a mistake putting me in a girl's body," or vice versa. In today's day and age, where censorship is gradually increasing, where anything goes, and "YOLO" is the motto to live by, few dare to correct such ideas.

As a Black man who grew up playing with white action-figures among four black sisters who played with white dolls, I recall feeling bad about the color of my skin. It was not just from playing with the toys but noticing the preferential treatment white people enjoyed and the admiration many received (for various things). I did not understand systemic racism enough to explain it, but I recall one time at about five or six years old, I told my mom "I wish I had been born white." Thankfully, she corrected me. I can imagine how much more disturbed she would have been had I convinced myself I was a white person in a black boy's body. Would this not have been utter confusion?

Back then, people were a bit more concerned with honesty than with political correctness, someone could have said I had a problem with my identity, and they would have been right. Thankfully, I had a good mother and not someone to feed me with cotton candy fluff. She did not twist wisdom and encourage the confusion by telling me "You can be whatever you want to be." Instead, my mom helped me to love myself, and she guided me to better understand and embrace my identity.

Nowadays, I understand this identity (of mine) better than ever! I am the spirit which God assigned to this body of mine. Additionally, I have the biological components of a man and I am called to be what God has assigned me to be. Therefore, I fully accept and embrace the responsibilities of masculinity (such as being the first line of physical defense for my family). Also, I am "heterosexual", because I *learned to be* (just as we all learn what we like). I cannot blame anyone for this. I was not born that way, for as a newborn, I never had sexual thoughts or feelings toward anyone; but as I developed, I **gained** those thoughts and sure there was some degree of guidance and instruction, but our first parents (Adam and Eve) were instructed to be fruitful and multiply. Through this, their descendants learned about reproduction.

Only God can define us, redeem us, and save us. We can only show defiance through failed efforts to redefine ourselves or what is morally upright. A man who thinks he is a woman, for instance or the reverse, has not redefined his or her identity. That would be like a computer thinking it is an airplane! No matter how "smart" it has become, its identity has already been determined by its maker. Likewise, ours has been determined and inscribed into the DNA of every one of our cells. A box is a box just as bed is a bed. A man is a man and women are women. God created our senses for perception, for us to identify what he created and defined. Therefore, it is a dishonest and deliberate act of confusion to call things what they are not; and confusion perpetuates greater lies and deceit.

Anything that conflicts with God's truth should not be allowed to infiltrate our minds, and those of our children. We should not be encouraged to participate in such lies. I (the author) refuse to call someone who is clearly a man—"a woman", "a duck", "a raccoon", or anything he is not. I will have respect for him as someone made after the likeness of God even if it is more than he has for himself. I refuse to call a woman something she is not. I will have more respect for her as someone made after the likeness of God even if it exceeds the respect she has for herself. Also, a singular entity is not plural except if there is more than one spirit within the individual. Therefore, it is preposterous to call some**_one_** "They" (as some propose). I digress.

It is disturbing that when good parents admonish **their** children in front of those who embrace rebellion, the parents are villainized. Meanwhile, school systems promote confusing thought patterns such as the existence of 50+ genders! They manipulate and corrupt young minds without reproach! What a travesty! There are certainly different levels of masculinity and femininity. Some men are more "macho" than others, and some women are "daintier" than others. Indeed, there is "fluidity" (if we wish to use that term) **_within_** the confines of the **boundaries**, God established! There just is none outside of that. Are we free to create our own lanes so to speak? Absolutely! However, there are paths that seem right to people, but those paths lead to cliffs and dead ends.

Sadly, belief in God and the Bible has come under heavy attack. The world teaches more and more people to reject our creator, which helps the next generation accept the grand delusion. As a result, they do not appreciate the awesome LORD of this universe, the wonderful plans, and purposes He has for us, and how we are fearfully and wonderfully made. Instead, they are educated to become part of a massive herd of sheep often led by corrupt shepherds. Further, they learn to depend on the promises of provision, and protection made by other human beings when they should, instead, trust God first and foremost.

We can see this more evidently today. In the year 2020, much changed in the world. Masses were so misled by media, false prophets, lying political figures, and rich "heroes" that they failed to see the amount of control they were surrendering to their crooked shepherds. A disease put the entire world in fear, but rather than turn to God for our great reset, we continued to trust people with our ultimate future. We continued to put faith in those who promoted their selfish interests. Many leaders who had done their part in bringing the world into its "new normal" especially in depravity also spearheaded the changes they felt would get us out of this mess. Like the increasing world debt, however, the downward spiral of decadence is a bottomless pit. Without a "great reset," of our souls where we submit ourselves before God and His righteousness, it will see no end. His way is better than ours, but if we do not change our course, and rid ourselves of selfishness and pride; in time, God will come with a reset of His own.

The world needs to do things God's way to prosper. There is no law God established to harm us. All His standards result in prosperity in different areas of our lives. In the book of Genesis, God gave mankind (through Adam and Eve) the purpose of caring for this world and ruling over it in righteousness. Righteousness comes from God. Had we kept our minds on godly things, we would not have to try and "save the environment," for waste would not have accumulated. Restaurants with excess food, cancelled orders, etc. would feed the poor before they fed the dumps. People would not live lives of excess pleasure and selfish comfort requiring enormous energy consumption and toxic emissions. We would not have to reform justice systems because every court decision would be reasonable for everyone, not just "the majority" and justice would always be served appropriately. Moreover, out of love for both God and others, people would turn away from evil such that lawsuits and prisons would disappear. We would not have to change the economy because all people (male and female) would be fairly compensated, etcetera. Our current systems reward the already rich while crushing the poor. This causes a disparity, which (in our current model) leads to covetousness (jealousy along with greed) and violence.

Poor men who yearn for extravagant lives, fancy cars, and "the women that come with them" often do desperately wicked and even violent things. Women who want lives of luxury and safety often look for men who can help them acquire such comforts. When both are in abject poverty, even their drive to survive brings out beasts from within.

If the world did things God's way, health and wellness would also abound. We have increasing need of doctors because our nutrition is lacking and instead of exercising, many sit behind computers and work with their fingers. Rest is also critical for good health, but instead of resting, we allow thoughts and worries to keep us up at night. Finally, our over-reliance on artificial remedies robs our bodies of opportunities to strengthen themselves.

Sometimes medication heals, sometimes it kills. Yet we put our faith in it more often than we should. Now and then those who skip the doctor's visit get worse and perhaps die in which case maybe they should have seen a doctor. Other times those who see their doctor get worse and may die, when they otherwise might have lived had they trusted God and their bodies. The lesson is this, doctors do not determine our lifespans. God already did. Many see doctors for ailments that their bodies could have recovered from. At best, they walk away with lighter pockets, or with a bill they cannot afford, but at worst, they walk away with a nosocomial (hospital acquired infection) or die. My point is this, while doctors can help in the healing process, health does not come from them, but from God and what He has created to sustain us (i.e. food, rest, immunity, etc.).

We are superlatively designed! Our immune systems far surpass any military response to even the most coordinated microbial attacks, yet if influential people tell entire nations they have to kill off every germ and virus around them (the very microbes that help strengthen our immune systems), they have been conditioned to succumb to fear without questioning their leaders. Lysol will sell out the next day! Everyone will tremble and hide. Few faithfully pray and trust in God and His incredible design.

In the year 2020, most of the world wanted to live in a bubble because they trusted man over God; but God never gave us a spirit of fear. Instead, we learned to be fearful when we exchanged the truth of God for lies. He made our bodies so phenomenal that even several thousand years ago when the stakes for our survival were purportedly higher, we thrived (even without hospitals)!

So why interfere now, especially seeing how our interference has caused so much damage to this world? If even the simplest cell is much more advanced than any one thing we have ever designed, what makes us think that now is the time for us to start helping Nature in her selective processes?

In our ignorance of God, our self-exaltation, and stubborn rebellion, we neglect how inexplicably majestic His designs are. We listen to other human beings, the so-called "great minds of this world", drooling, as they attempt to explain the natural world to us with words that fail to capture its endless wonders. We elevate them as though they were gods, but they are mere mortals who exist as a single period in a thousand paged book. Though they thought they could comprehend the book during their short stint, they were merely specks that could not contain the enormity of what they beheld. Even their teams for generations failed to grasp the knowledge and wisdom surrounding them.

Everyone has lied at some point or another, but when lying influencers speak, many people imagine hearing nothing but the truth. Oh, how sad we become when we drift from the knowledge of God, for no matter how upsetting the truth may be, it is appointed for everyone to die once and then face judgement. This will happen. Crooked leaders can try to silence those who speak the truth. They usually consider the Bible and any book inspired by its doctrines to be dangerous literature. Such people know the truth has the power to ultimately disrupt their agendas.

Deceptive powers have not just infiltrated the school system and governments, but also "the church." In fact, to be quite honest, one can say their influence began in the church, then spread to governments, and finally school systems. There are rulers of darkness in this world who perform spiritual wickedness in high places and hate God. Why else would they find a Biblical worldview threatening? More evidence favors a creator, over a random explosion, yet so many Godly scientists have disproportionally been laid off for daring to challenge the secular paradigm. Most people are not ready for the truth because acknowledging God changes **everything,** and we often dislike change.

What's He like? If His Kingdom is so extraordinary, how can we live in such a place? What must we do? What must we give up? What does He want from our lives? What are our purposes? Why has He been so quiet? Does He speak through people? Does He really care for us? For the record, the answer to the last question is YES; and so much more than we can imagine!

CHAPTER 9
Let God Be True

For much of my life, I was unaware of the two kinds of science that currently exist—the pure, legitimate type (real knowledge which experimentation *can* prove) and so-called "theoretical science." To be fair, some conjectures of theoretical science have been proven true, and those theories subsequently became fact, but others cannot be proven. Still, *the only kind* of "science" that conflicts with the Bible is **always** the unprovable theoretical type. The secular model of universal origin fits within the realm of the unprovable.

Pure science and even history support Biblical accounts. On the other hand, pseudoscience is exposed by Biblical truth. Therefore, the only ways to ensure the acceptance of the secular worldview are to ban the Bible from schools and other public institutions and infiltrate the church. Still, truth does not change.

The observed evidence of the collective human experience suggests that **every** functional system, machine, and device has or had a maker. We know an abandoned house had a maker. the buildings at Chernobyl had makers; a lost flashlight in the middle of the woods was made. The real world requires the use of real reason, not the train of thought most of us have boarded in school just to pass our classes. We should not forget to get off this imaginary train when it is no longer useful.

Do you not know your body is a machine? I am asking you, dear reader. Do you not realize that scale for scale, we cannot even come close to surpassing what God created? Some have convinced themselves there is no God, but virtually every shred of evidence that Big Bang theorists and Evolutionists **_misinterpret_** (they do this often) is truly evidence of God's handiwork.

We are marvels of engineering who also have creative abilities. We can make humanoid robots in our image while imagining that 50 years from now they will be even more like us. Most people have seen Hollywood movies about advanced humanoid robots (i.e. Terminator, I-robot, Ex Machina), and have been impressed with a hope that one day robots will be as advanced as movie depictions. They have no idea how exceedingly superlative we are compared to anything humanity can even dream of making.

Artificial intelligence may seem to have approximated average human intelligence and, in some ways, even surpassed it, but our mental capacity is only one aspect of our design. Comprehensively, we are unparalleled by our contraptions. Scale for scale, we are still a whole lot smarter than machines. They are not even close!

As cases in point, Google Assistant, Alexa, and Siri may appear to know a lot, but their "intelligence" comes from servers occupying entire rooms while our CPU is smaller than a soccer ball! Still, our brains can process enough real-time information to overload many of the world's most powerful computers! God may not have designed us just to perform complex computations, but we process bewildering amounts of information at any given time.

To put our complexity in better perspective, the internet, a highly impressive human achievement which virtually spans the world is not even half as incredible as the network within our bodies. Let's imagine a year from now, Siri (Apple Inc.'s IOS) were given a body and her brain became the combined power of all the servers that support her current capabilities, she would quickly learn that her ability to retrieve information from her database to answer her curious users is vastly easier than learning how to catch a ball while in motion (i.e. running, walking, or riding a bike). She would also learn how inferior her body was if she ever had a localized short circuit. Unlike us, she would not have repair cells to fix bodily damage. She would frequently need to power down and recharge because lithium ion battery packs are not nearly as efficient as the human battery.

In the human body, our energy does not come from our hearts, other organs, or battery packs. The heart itself, for the sake of simplicity, is merely a smart-pump which is powered by something else, —<u>our entire bodies</u> which are replete with cells that metabolize food! In other words, and not to be redundant, our bodies are the batteries that power our bodies and we recharged them with the food we eat. We do not need to plug ourselves into a wall. We can eat on the go!

Blood flows throughout our bodies delivering oxygen, nutrients, and energy to every organ. Every cell contains energy banks in organelles called mitochondria! Therefore, we have no need for battery packs. Our blood alone carries so much energy throughout our bodies that it is no wonder the Bible says, "life is in the blood." Additionally, as it travels within us it dissipates body heat to help stabilize our temperatures. If Siri had a body, she would easily overheat trying to keep up with a human being. If she experienced a wi-fi issue, she would lag and glitch. She would not be able to develop adaptable immunity against small micromechanical threats without highly intelligent cells to defend her. Shall I continue?

Dear reader, if you are on the wrong train, you are headed in the wrong direction. Most people who have boarded the academic trains of thought have remained on its circular track. I am glad God showed me He is here in the real world and cannot be found in a world of falsities. I now see the works of His invisible hands for the unsurpassable marvels they are, but one day I will see Him face to face. This I declare in the name of Jesus, my Lord and you can too.

Knowing what we know (based on observable evidence), not what we have been conditioned to accept, why do we dare take credit from God? Theoretical astrophysicists and biologists imagine their famous "primordial soup" coming together by itself, yet their experiments do not reflect that. They lie to themselves and to others. What soup has ever made itself? Such a meal would come in handy for those who are bedridden! Instead of tossing random ingredients together to see if they can become something meaningful on their own, these theorists speculate in probabilities. They have perplexed themselves with theoretical jargon, and labyrinthine ways of thinking, trapping themselves in their prideful intellects. It is incredible they have forgotten a fundamental rule of probability; —**it is derived from known possibilities!**

The chance of a two-sided balanced coin landing on either side is approximately 1:2 or 50%. Sure, there is a tiny probability it may land on its edge, but we say it is roughly 50% because the known possibilities are as follows:

- it will land heads (roughly 50% of the time)
- it will land tails (roughly 50% of the time)
- it will land on its side (those odds are so slim they are not even worth calculating)

We know for fact, however, that without some external force acting upon it, a flipped coin will not freeze-float in the air. Likewise, we know the probability of a 6-sided dice landing on any one side is 1:6 or 16.66...%. We know this because there are only 6 known possibilities. Now the chance of something fully functional assembling itself, however, —or appearing out of nowhere, —is 0%. Based on the collective human observation of reality, it is impossible, and therefore improbable! Let God be true.

CHAPTER 10
Misread Evidence

The Bible predicted long ago that many would exchange the truth of God for a lie; the lie that we are insignificant, and that the universe is the **only** functional and orderly system that created itself. They would argue that it came about without God and that it is not orderly at all, but violent and chaotic. They would shift blame from themselves to God, saying, "if He exists, He did not really create an orderly world," when in fact, *we* (human beings) *are all to blame* for refusing to live how He commanded us to. We have brought the disorder. The Book of Romans says it best in Chapter 1 verses 22-25:

(22) **Professing themselves to be wise**, they became fools, (23) and changed the glory of the incorruptible God into an image made like to corruptible man, and birds, and four-footed beasts, and creeping things. (24)Therefore God also gave them up to uncleanness through the lusts of their hearts, to dishonor their own bodies between themselves:(25)Who changed the truth of God into a lie, and worshiped and served the creature more than the Creator, who is blessed forever. Amen

To profess means to affirm (or state as fact) a faith in something or allegiance to that something. For instance, one who professes Christ affirms a belief in the one who died for all sins. As another example, a person who professes the theory of Evolution is one who declares that their faith lies in that theory. It is disheartening that those who affirm unproven theories have also claimed themselves to be wise, but God calls them the opposite. The Bible also says they teach others to do the same. They have become ***profess***ors in schools and universities, shaping the minds of future generations, not to look to God, but to search everywhere else.

Schools are increasingly banning bibles. For reasons related to bias and contempt, school systems generally reject the Bible as an authority in truth. Apart from God, we tend to err and become foolish. In the pursuit of so-called "knowledge", many have exchanged the truth for what is false because they have learned to perceive the former as a nuisance while the latter scratches their itching ears. Dear reader, to know is not to speculate. Do not be deceived. The fact that science has brought us modern technology does not automatically make human knowledge infallible, nor human intentions honorable. Remember, every one of us is flawed. We all sin and without God, we tend to work selfishly. When we do good unto others, it is not always out of genuine love, but out of self-centered karmic expectation. We can do better if we let God show us how.

There is only one infallible being, and He is not the one who is causing people to disobey their parents, lie, cheat, steal, then grin like it is all good and then shrug his shoulders nonchalantly. He is not shooting up schools and churches, kidnapping people, and murdering them. He is not the one attacking every moral fiber of society and encouraging vagary. He is not continually redacting science and history because of His errors, uncertainty, and insecurity. No God is very secure and does not change. A being who knows all does not need to learn and accept new ideas. Since we are not omniscient, we are susceptible to deception, misinformation, and manipulation. God wants us to wake up! He says in the Bible "My people perish for lack of knowledge." -(Hosea 4:6)

God is unchanging. He does not replace structure and boundaries with "fluidity" wherever separation is needed. We know that if a house were built with fluid walls, pillars, and beams it would be nothing more than a roof in a puddle. It would not stand. Therefore, who would want to live in a place without structure (organization, order, boundaries, rooms, etc.) and separation (from the elements and danger, noises, etc.)? A critical error of the carnal mind lies in thinking, "God must not want me to be free" when the truth is quite the opposite. God gives freedom (with some clear rules and boundaries). Conversely, sin and lies often imprison people.

For this reason, God says, "The truth shall set you free." Sex, for instance is not off-limits, but God intended for married couples who genuinely love each other to enjoy this level of pleasure and intimacy. It was supposed to be a perk of being married. Doing it this way would have drastically prevented heartbreak, family disintegration, family dysfunction, STDs and STIs, etc. Likewise, God is not against wine. However, if you wish to drink, stay aware, and mentally sharp. Do not get drunk. This concept makes sense for safety and self-defense. A drunkard and his family are easy targets for a criminal. Drunkards also have impaired judgment and may become verbally, emotionally, or physically abusive. There are many more reasons why self-control is necessary, but hopefully, you get the point.

Instead of looking at the one tree, they could not eat from, Adam and Eve should have looked at all the available ones. You see, God had provided a single boundary, but all around that boundary was freedom to choose without consequence. They did what is now synonymous with our humanity; they sinned, but we do not have to remain prisoners to the power of sin. Christ died so that we could choose life.

The **theory** of evolution is superficially sound and even attractive (to the untrained ear). It does not require proof since this extremely sluggish phenomenon supposedly occurs outside of the possibilities of human perception. How convenient! There is no proof, and yet evolutionists want their followers to have *faith* that this unseen phenomenon occurs. These theoretical scientists persuade many to believe that one microorganism randomly came into existence—fully formed and somehow programmed (purportedly by no one) to survive and thrive.

Somehow, this microbe knew it had to self-divide in time to ensure its survival, and many views this to be more palatable than the truth, which declares God made all things! Disliking the idea of an All-powerful God with unwavering righteousness and a set of laws that are (at times) difficult to abide by (and undoubtedly impossible not to break occasionally) does not make a reality that created itself more likely. We can believe someone engineered our realm, or we can continue speculating it just popped into existence. Choosing the latter, however, is foolish.

Someone far more advanced in intellect and power than ourselves created everything we can and cannot see. Furthermore, this creator programmed their biological functions and development with genetic **code**. Though this code is evidence of creation, it has been misrepresented by many scientists who reason that numerous kinds of animals appear to be related to others. This argument is quite fascinating because, in our engineering, we imitate what exists in nature. Besides, as creative as we human beings might be, our "creations" <u>also</u> appear to be related! Family sedans, large SUVs, and semi-trucks, for instance, are related. They all belong to the family of automobiles. They have four or more wheels, two or more doors, and storage compartments (trunks or trailers) of various sizes. They all have windshields, headlights, and many other similarities. Yet one would be unwise to say that any of these vehicles evolved from another. They are more similar to each other than to boats and aircraft, but we know they share common makers—human beings! They did not just pop into existence. Nothing in our visible realm ever does.

Similarities in genetic code are not the result of evolution, nor are they evidence of it. Instead, they are evidence of a common programming language just as JavaScript and Python have been used for many computers. Unfortunately, such claims to promote evolutionary theory are baseless. In fact, out of all fossils we have unearthed, of animals assumed to be related to other kinds, there are so-called "missing links" between not one, two, or even a few of them,—but between them **all**! Not one selection of fossil evidence shows animals in transition (such as pigs growing wings or fish tails). Even when aberrations appear (such as people with six fingers), nature has always corrected itself, and life remains within the parameters outlined by the Master Designer (God). In other words, human beings, in general, will <u>never</u> adapt to have a sixth finger. To see the terrible flaws in the theory of evolution, let us analogize creation to two human innovations a smartphone and a tablet.

A modern smart phone did not evolve from a tablet or vice versa (perhaps the concept of it did in some way), but human beings designed both. Nevertheless, the operating systems may be similar due to a shared information language(s) used to program them. By the same token, all life is based on genetic **code** just as all modern computers function using **code**. Code does not develop in a vacuum, nor can chaos form it. That would be as improbable as a fall breeze blowing fallen leaves into a message that says, "Autumn is here." Why would anyone believe such nonsense?

When unprovable theories are forced upon others by those who reject the bible and teach others to do the same, many will feel as though they must believe the lie. Everybody needs something to believe. The curious nature of the spirit compels it to seek out its origin, but as most people study the prevailing scientific worldview of our time, the black hole of deception pulls them further from the knowledge of God.

THE WAGES OF SIN

The debate over the origin of worlds is not a matter of "Science" versus "Religion." In fact, the first scientists were believers in God! No, this debate is a conflict of paradigms. It is a clash of views.

I am not counting on this book to change the predominantly faithless worldview of scientists, although such an event would be cause for rejoicing. I am appealing to those who realize the truth in everything I have said thus far. I am calling to those who no longer want to be manipulated by lies which the community of false scientists continues to redact, —assumptions which, for some reason, are exempt from thorough examination under the application of the Scientific Method. The truth of God has not changed, nor will it ever. Unlike the Big Bang theory and the theory of Evolution, it stands up to scrutiny, but it is uncomfortable for those who are new to it. It is like a bright light greeting newly woken eyes.

Many animals do indeed resemble each other—or rather, similar blueprints that God used to create them. —but not because of evolutionary events. Rather, they share the information language that God used to build life on Earth. So, if the DNA of one organism resembles that of another, it is because the information is related to itself. C++ is similar to C++. Likewise, JavaScript is like JavaScript. Therefore, it stands to reason that DNA is related to DNA!

DNA establishes the parameters in which physical characteristics and (physical) identity express themselves. Thus, even if we miniaturize a dog breed, for instance, until it resembles a mouse, it will <u>never</u> evolve into a mouse because its DNA makes it a dog. Therefore, even the tiniest dog will never be able to reproduce with a mouse without some sort of genetic sabotage. It will always reproduce only *according to its kind,* as the Bible has already made clear. Barring scientific intervention, animals will only procreate with their kind. A wolf can mate with a golden retriever and have puppies, but lions cannot procreate with zebras (not that they would want to). Instead, they are reproductively compatible with their biological kind, which includes tigers.

When the LORD instructed Noah to bring two pairs of each animal, He knew about the laws of ***adaptation***. Reproduction leads to the procreation of similar life forms after their kind, but it does not replicate life forms. God designed Adam and Eve as distinct individuals who would reproduce *distinguishable* offspring. God did not need millions of replicas. He wanted diversity, and sure enough, some of Adam and Eve's descendants were darker in complexion, some were lighter, some were taller, others shorter. As for the diversity of animals, it came from reproducing distinct offspring.

Many consider adaptation to be an observable glimpse of evolutionary forces. That notion, however, is incorrect. Adaptation within genetically specified parameters makes sense because attributes like physicality and speed can be improved through exercise. We know muscles can become more accustomed to bearing greater weight and more efficient at performing repeated motions. Therefore, musculature, physicality, and general appearance can change, but within predetermined limits.

There is a critical difference between **evidence** and **proof**, and if evidence is appropriately and consistently analyzed, all "scientific" theories conflicting with the bible will remain theories. They will remain figments of the imaginations of those in opposition to God's truth and legitimate supremacy over all creation. Missing links will remain missing because creatures cannot escape the identity God gave them.

Only one pair of original large wildcats was needed to bring about the various species of lions, tigers, panthers, and leopards that exist today. Likewise, only one pair of original wolves was required to bring about every wolf species as well as <u>EVERY</u> dog breed that exists. For those who did not know, all dogs (Rottweilers, German Shepherds, Chihuahuas, etc. came from wolves). In like manner, only one pair of humans are responsible for every ethnicity and every individual who has ever lived! Evolution is one big convoluted lie.

The flood is not an event that took place an absurdly long time ago. All flood accounts were written by people who had not bought into the false religions of "the Big Bang" and "Evolution." They were not written by people who speculated that the earth was billions of years old. Ancient scribes did not use the notoriously inaccurate method of carbon-dating to guess the age of the earth. They believed the earth was much younger than most influential scientists proclaim.

Nowadays, many people scoff at the notion that earth may only be thousands of years old! They have been fed lies for so long. Moreover, they have learned it is ridiculous to think otherwise. Therefore, they are inclined to ridicule those who refuse to believe modern theories over the words of their ancestors. If flood stories were local events, then why did so many of their protagonists spend considerable time building floating vessels? Why didn't they simply migrate? Also, if the worldwide flood truly happened during human history (without the convenient multi-billion-year timeframe required for evolution, how did life resurge after the flood? Keep in mind evolutionists believe it took billions of years for one cell to become everything we know. Dear reader, if you must question everything, then question everything fairly.

Many professors teach there's evidence for the Big bang theory and evolution. Be careful when you hear that. Evidence alone is not proof. For instance, a fingerprint at a crime scene is indeed evidence. However, it does not immediately confirm the owner of the print committed the crime in question. While it can reasonably make him or her a suspect, the fingerprint only proves that the suspect touched the surface upon which it was found. Proper use of evidence can expose a criminal, and enough evidence can assist in the proving of criminality. But evidence itself is **not** proof!

Likewise, the evidence that rock layers can result from sedimentary deposits over long periods is not proof that earth is billions of years old. There is plenty of evidence that catastrophic events can alter landscapes and topography, both drastically and rapidly. Such events (like the eruption of Mt Saint Helen's and the drastic topographical change that ensued) have occurred countless times in the history of the earth. Therefore, sedimentary layering only *proves* nature's ability to bury evidence slowly through normal processes or quickly through natural disasters. Now that we have completed this detour, let's get back to the great flood!

CHAPTER 11
The Accuracy of the Biblical Flood Account

The account of Noah is unique and proves itself. Other stories only bear a superficial resemblance to the Judao-Christian account but are riddled with differences. Aside from their discrepancies, the inconsistencies and continuity issues of other accounts make them much less believable than the biblical one. For instance, though many involve the construction of a watercraft (i.e., boat or ark), most do not address the issue of post-diluvian repopulation, and the ones that do *cannot* be supported by science. Allow me to share a few examples.

The Greek story of Deucalion and Pyrrha only accounts for the survival and resurgence of people but not animals. After surviving the great flood, Deucalion and his wife, Pyrrha, are said to have thrown rocks and stones behind them, and as they did, the rocks and stones became people. Science cannot confirm such a phenomenon, but at least at that time, it gave its believers a modicum of closure as to how human beings resurged. I suppose 'good ol' fashion mating' was out of the question. It would have been too obvious! Besides, most people almost expect "religion" to oppose science.

The Hindu myth of Manu and the flood also does not explain the resurgence of animal life on earth, for Manu only took people aboard his small boat, which begs the question, "How did land animals resurge?" The Sumerian legend of Utnapishtim, which (superficially) is one of the closest to the Judao-Christian account of Noah and the great flood, also leaves something to be desired. It explains how the protagonist (Utnapishtim) carried with him the seed of all living things. Furthermore, it sounds somewhat ambiguous and utterly impossible for a human being to have carried out. How would one go about acquiring the seeds of all living things (many of which are invisible without a microscope), then organizing them, and controlling temperatures before artificial incubation ever existed? Further, with what would the protagonist have fertilized the plethora of seeds he had collected?

Only the Bible preserves and presents the Flood account in a scientifically sound way. In fact, real scientists have unearthed ample evidence of a worldwide flood. Too bad "trolls" exist in the scientific community and in the media; otherwise, the world would have known this. Therefore, when I speak of real scientists, I refer to practitioners of the discipline of questioning and hypothesizing without biases, to those who experiment and test every theory. When I speak of real scientists, I mean the ones who do not accept any theory as fact until it is proven. Real scientists practice sound reasoning and observation skills. They genuinely seek the truth **no matter where it leads**, and they share accurate results. The Big Bang is not fact, but it seems acceptable enough to entice itching ears who will fight to support this deception.

The only way to trick someone is if they do not know the truth. If the Big Bang happened without a Supreme Intellect having first existed outside of the very time and space He is said to have created, then we should not have to use contraptions (such as the famous Hadron collider) to try and recreate this theoretical phenomenon. If it happened by itself, then we should be able to observe other examples of things that happen without stimuli. After all, the scientific method was built on a principle that science (which is knowledge) should be reliable and that repeated experiments should bring about consistent results. In trying to create a Big Bang, we are altering the conditions under which this supposed "accident" occurred. We are suggesting that perhaps, a Big Bang needed help after all, but this time we will play God. In that case, should we not at least speculate that He triggered the cosmic explosion by smashing atoms together in His even larger collider, or perhaps He's just God, and He did not need anything but his omnipotence and words that obey and carry out His will!

Nobody needs a doctorate to know without a shadow of a doubt that random finished products do not appear out of thin air. In the beginning, God created the Heavens and the earth—PERIOD. The truth is clear, short, and sweet. It saves the time, energy, and resources like money which people would otherwise waste. We have wasted billions of dollars pumping them into the very institutes that feed us lies mixed in with enough truth to become believable! It is sad.

The Heavens and earth did not originate from an infinitely dense, marble-sized gravitational singularity of space, time, and incalculable mass which so happened to explode due to any number of internal and random conditional changes such as energy and gravitational fluctuations which resulted in a domino effect that has led us to this moment (you can inhale now). It sounds "highly intelligent" when a scientist says such a thing. Quite frankly, it is incredibly absurd and unscientific to treat such an unsound theory as a fact. It certainly sounds like science to someone with a bias toward God, but if we established anything in "The Serpent's Lie," it is that God uses science and science supports the existence of God. The fact that the sun releases energy which can be recaptured by photovoltaic cells is science. We have observed that plants do this and found other evidence that suggested that light and heat are energy. Experiments proved our theories, and they became science because they were valid, reliable, and repeatable. However, this modern idea that the world and everything around are is the **_only_** functional systems lacking a creator and moral authority (who superseded all) is one hundred percent ludicrous!

The theory that it took billions of years for the earth to form is not real science since the very foundation of that theory is flawed. Every event and every effect have a cause. A Big Bang, therefore, would not only require fuel (potential energy) but a spark from something or someone to release its immeasurably explosive force.

To set the record straight, here is what we know and have observed. Complex functional systems **are all designed**. Anyone who has ever seen anything physical and functional appear out of nowhere at any point in their life should really testify about it. I would greatly encourage you to shed light on this phenomenon. As for myself and everyone else who at least have one decent and honest eye, we have never witnessed such an event. There is not a single chance that anything random ever happens. Even seemingly random events have causes. Not even a hair ever appears out of nowhere. Therefore, talk of some kind of "primordial soup" from which all life supposedly originated should beg the question—who was the chef? If we are going to use analogies to 'dumb things down' for people without doctorate degrees in imaginary science, then let us at least keep it consistent. A primordial someone had to have made that primordial soup. No exception for this axiom exists. Dear reader, do not be misled. Real science must be observable because real science is knowledge and real knowledge ultimately knows God. What we know and accept as factual should be based on examples we have seen.

The Bible states God created the world. Generations later, however, He caused the world-wide flood to destroy almost every living thing because human beings had become incredibly wicked, angels and humans mingled, and violence was ubiquitous on the earth. It is not difficult to see that as good and righteous as we (human beings <u>can</u> be), <u>we tend to deviate</u> from God's intended plans for humanity. God has not changed, but people do, and over time, boundaries between right and wrong become blurred by our flawed reasoning. We play "devil's advocate" and suppose our errors are not so bad if we compare them to another person's faults, or even a worse alternative ("the greater of two evils").

Additionally, we often determine (from our vantage point) that our actions have had no negative impact on anyone else.

The flood must have killed all land animals (even the ones that could swim for some time). No matter which account you read, the deluge lasted for several days to several months. Even the best swimming land animals would eventually have drowned in such conditions. Soon afterward, life resurged, but who restored the human and animal populations? Was it the Greek Deucalion and his wife Pyrrha (who tossed shape-shifting rocks behind themselves—rocks that became people)? Was it Manu (who had only taken other people aboard his boat)? Could it have been Utnapishtim (who carried the seeds of all life with him)—or was it Noah whose God had created animals male and female to reproduce after their kind and required him to use that *observable and repeatable cycle* of mating and reproduction? Without bias, it should be the account of Noah for the account still makes sense today. Additionally, scientific evidence such as geological rock formations and fossils especially those found in the Grand Canyon and similar locations, supports the flood account of Noah.

CHAPTER 12
The Great Deluge

A worldwide flood indeed occurred in ancient times, and the Biblical account (in Genesis) provides the best explanation for humanity's survival and the resurgence of all other life. When God commanded Noah to bring two of every kind of animal, he was not asking him to bring two of every species of land animal that we know of today. If God asked someone to save all dogs by fitting them into a four-door sedan, someone could accomplish this feat by saving the purest male and female wolves they could find! After all, every dog breed descended from wolves. There were no golden retrievers, pitbulls, or German shepherds in Noah's day. Likewise, all the animals that we know of today came from an ancestral **kind**.

Gen 6:19-20 *"And of every living thing of all flesh, two of every sort shalt thou bring into the ark, to keep them alive with thee; they shall be male and female. Of fowls after their kind, and of cattle after their kind, of every creeping thing of the earth after his kind, two of every sort shall come unto thee, to keep them alive."*

Throughout the 120-year grace period, God stayed in touch with Noah to keep him informed. One week from the flood, God spoke with Noah saying:

"For yet seven days, and I will cause it to rain upon the earth forty days and forty nights; and every living substance that I have made will I destroy from off the face of the earth." Gen 7:4

When the time finally came, Noah and his family boarded the ark with a pair of every animal kind God had instructed him to gather, and the LORD shut the door of the Ark. Shortly after that came the fierce downpour.

Not one person outside of Noah's family had repented during the 120-year grace period the LORD gave. Suddenly, cries of distress began to break out from all around the ark. Countless people (who up to that point had mocked the LORD and His servant Noah) were now crying out to them for salvation. It is not hard to imagine this dismal scene once you understand the power of a near-death experience to make people suddenly remember God exists. In hopeless situations, many recall the presence of a Supreme Being whom they can cry out to for mercy, forgiveness, healing, and salvation. In the case of those who the great flood engulfed, they screamed for another chance! Regrettably, the LORD had been merciful and patient long enough. Their time was up.

For forty days and forty nights, the ark rocked upon turbulent waters, which were so high that they covered the highest mountains. All land-dwelling life except the ones aboard the ark were exterminated. Several weeks later, God shut the floodgates of heaven and the fountains of the deep. The rain slowed to a stop, and the waters subsided. Eventually, the ark came to rest upon the dry ground. When it was safe to do so, the LORD opened the door of the ark, and every life that He had preserved trickled out from it. In gratitude for the salvation that he had received from the LORD, Noah made an offering to Him.

CHAPTER 13
Last Great Flood

Genesis 8:21 - 22

21 And the Lord smelled a sweet savor, and the Lord said in his heart, I will not again curse the ground any more for man's sake, for the imagination of man's heart is evil from his youth; neither will I again smite any more everything living as I have done.

After the flood, God told Noah it would be the last time He would ever curse the ground for human sin. He did not remove the original curse from it but promised never to add to it. Our Heavenly Father knew the wretched state of humanity—that we were ill-fated to be born, grow up, then procreate into cycles of sin. Even so, He saw something special in us from before time began. He does not forsake those who believe in Him even when they turn from Him. Instead, the LORD shows mercy and calls us back to Him.

The decline of society appears to follow a thermodynamic principle called the "law of entropy," which suggests that order devolves into chaos over time. Many people wonder why issues such as racism, sexism, and hate, have not disappeared in the 21st century. The honest answer is that it does not matter what generation we are a part of. We are up against forces that are beyond us, powers, and principalities that are far older than we often consider. We are not clothed with the glory Adam and Eve had before their fall, and most importantly, to our detriment, most of the world does not follow the will of the LORD as it pertains to living righteously.

Dear reader, there is still hope for people in this world. It was always in God's plan that everything we have seen would come to pass. Even so, He wants to fix our brokenness. He does not desire to see people perish, but for them to acknowledge their wickedness and repent. That is a step of humility. It's not humble to think we're "good" when the reality is we have all lied, cheated, stolen, hurt people, ignored the oppressed, gossiped, shown impatience, unforgiveness, entitlement, and hopefully you get the point. Sadly, in a realm of over seven billion people, each with their own free will, not everyone will humble themselves and seek the LORD.

Modern society is becoming increasingly desensitized to sin. The road to recovery always begins by first identifying problems and admitting that they are, in fact, problems. The challenge, however, is that we often do not want to call a spade exactly what it is, especially in our "PC culture." These days if a spade thinks it is a diamond, "who cares? How does that affect the game?"—If a man thinks he is a woman, for instance, his confusion is viewed as his business and no one else's. In fact, the world villainizes anyone who dares to challenge such confusion. But those who accept it and fail to stand their moral ground only maintain superficial friendships built upon lies. Relationships built on indifference lack genuine love. "Well, as long as they're not hurting anyone..."

Newsflash,—if you are a parent, sibling, another family member, or friend, please heed the following words:

That extraordinary, fearfully, and wonderfully made human being who struggles with homosexuality or gender confusion will face the consequences sooner or later if you remain indifferent. You can love people without being an "enabler." The consequences of their lifestyles may not be immediately apparent, but they are certain. I do not advise for you to be harsh or insensitive. Rather, be patient. Do not threaten to disown them, for our Heavenly Father has not disowned anyone for their sins (not while His grace can still be found). Instead, He has reached out to us, therefore you should do the same with your loved one(s) who are lost in sin— and be honest. Every sin has consequences. For instance, sexual immorality introduced the world to STDs and STIs.

Fornicators and adulterers are more likely to contract and spread venereal diseases. Likewise, the homosexual community, has a greater predisposition to certain health risks (namely among the men in this group). It is no coincidence, therefore, that those who practice sexual immorality are more likely to contract venereal diseases. Homosexuals in particular are more likely to contract hepatitis A, B, and C; HPV, anal caner, and a multitude of other STDs including HIV. According to the laws of statistics, numbers (in large enough sample sizes) do not lie. Granted, every person has free will to choose their way; please remember the paths we take may feel good at the time but the wrong ones lead to self-destruction.

Aberrant behaviors (even those "normalized" by certain influencers) are still such. They are behaviors that become patterns and even addictions. All habits are formed progressively and tend to increase in frequency when they are not controlled. Alcoholism, for instance, always starts with one drink. Drug addiction invariably begins with the first puff or hit. Thieves kick off their criminal careers by stealing one item. Serial murderers begin with one act of psychopathy. Fornicators begin by having sex with someone they were not married to and then they're hooked.

But imagine if all human beings learned to control their desires, and we respected and obeyed the Lord our God? Imagine if the world did this instead of seeking to defy His laws at every turn. What if all parents knew the LORD, honored, and followed Him, lived uprightly, and taught their children to do the same? Envision the type of realm we would live in if people got married and sincerely loved one another with an intensity and honesty that would stand the test of a lifetime. Imagine if every single person on earth experienced what it was like to live in a stable home and live the love-filled life that God has always desired for us from the beginning. How would our world look?

If we all did things God's way, everyone would honor their parents for raising them in safe homes filled with love and care. Every citizen of the world would recognize that their fellow person bears the image and likeness of the Most High. As a result, each would respect the other. None would bear false witness against anyone else. Justice would always be fair. None would covet, steal, cheat, kill, rape, assault, or even verbally abuse another.

We know murder is a horrific sin caused by pure hatred or fear. Fornication is a sin originating from the lust of the flesh. Adultery is a form of fornication that can damage the relationship between married couples and even devastate entire families. Stealing causes an unfair advantage for one party while creating an immediate setback for another. Lying demonstrates fear of facing the consequences deserved for a misdeed. Lying on someone else makes the other person bear responsibility for the trespass they did not commit. Coveting is wrong because it can lead to theft, lying, fornication, adultery, and even murder. God commanded us all to refrain from committing these sins, yet we practice them daily and wonder why the world is so awry. If we did things God's way, life would be much better.

Sadly, most people do not follow God. Instead, we have a mentality of "anything goes" and fail to realize the direct correlation between that mentality and the increasing power of the spiritual darkness enshrouding this world... ALL have sinned and fallen short of God's glory, but this fact should not cause us to give up our moral ideals, for, without those, we'd have no point of reference to comprehend morality and speak out against immorality. As a side note, those who love righteousness should be able to speak out without being shamed or made afraid. Let us be careful to note that speaking against these things does not equate to hating anyone.

Nowadays, part of our sinful condition lies in our lost identity. Humanity has forgotten God made us in His image. Society has exchanged the truth of God for a lie and sees itself as insignificant (merely a speck in an infinite universe). To the world, if God is real, then He, "She," or "It" is a force who could care less about humankind. Since human beings are allegedly "insignificant," one of the lies, we started to tell ourselves is that what we do is also insignificant, especially if it does not (immediately) hurt others.

Today, people are afraid to call a spade a spade. They are okay letting spades think they are diamonds and even cheer them on. The spades find people who say they care, but when we allow lies to continue, no matter how small, we do not show concern, we show apathy. Anyone who does not try to tell their friend the truth does not care as much as they should or is not considering the possible consequences. They do not delight in the ideal called "honesty," but instead enjoy the comfort of having avoided a tough conversation and the resentment that may or may not have ensued. That is how the "my truth," "your truth," "their truth" fallacy began.

If people get offended even over a truth we communicated in love, then we tend to treat their emotional response as seriously as a physical injury. From then on, we start walking on eggshells so to speak in order to avoid hurting their soft skin. There is no such thing as alternative truth or personal truth. There is only <u>the truth</u>, the lies we start believing in our minds, and the uncertainty we accept when we do not want to confront reality. People who experience any sort of identity confusion, for instance, should find those who **genuinely** want to help them face the absolute truth. Nowadays, however, to avoid ruffling feathers, many people will let a fellow human being think he is a bird. They will support this madness by saying, "well, it's his truth." But what if "his truth" possesses him to jump off a cliff with false confidence that he will fly? What if the poor and confused soul injures himself or worse, simply because others were too afraid he would dislike them for being honest (instead of supporting "his truth").

These days, many people do not know how to balance love with conviction and moral integrity. Moral integrity does not mean bending when the truth makes someone cry. It means that even when it hurts to see that person cry, we maintain our values. We do not have to agree with someone's lifestyle to love them! We merely have to make sure that even when we do approach them with the truth, we respect their free will, for even God has respected our free will up to this point and will continue to do so until the day of His return.

If a spade thinks it is a diamond, a few other spades may be inspired to follow suit. Though the spade thinks it is not affecting anyone else, its actions have a ripple effect. Since it perceives its actions as harmless, it spreads the same perception to others. Some diamonds even become confused. "If this spade is a diamond, then what am I?" We should understand that one person's error can lead to more confusion if we do not identify it, hold it up to the light of truth, and deal with it.

This parable applies to many things. It applies to gender identity confusion, age identity confusion, and even sexual orientation. Now, this is not an attempt to tell anyone how they "must" live their lives, who they "must" identify themselves as, or who they "must" fall in love with. Everyone is free to do as they will, but not every choice we make will be the right one, especially when we give in to sinful desires. Therefore, if we can be honest without defensiveness, self-victimization, or any sort of contextual distortion, I will say that the moral fibers of society are coming apart as we pretend that no one is affected by our sins. If God were to recreate the world and re-establish His boundaries, those boundaries would not change even if "times changed." God's unwavering integrity bothers many; for if He enjoyed partying, getting wasted, getting high, fornicating, "cussing" etc., his fan base would be a lot larger.

If the opposite of love is indifference, to quote Nobel Peace Prize winner Elie Wiesel, then one should not say they love a person while being indifferent toward their lifestyle. I never suggest that we impose our lifestyles upon others, but we certainly should not encourage self-destructive behavior. Honesty is **not** hatred.

If we do not shape up, our world will become more chaotic. Order is supposed to subject chaos to wisdom and virtue, at least under divine and perfect leadership. Unfortunately, chaos abounds in our modern world. This chaos is the result of apathy toward sin, lack of accountability, fear of honest discussion, and our general tendency to rebel against the ordinances of God. If the law of entropy (concerning society) is as predictable a trend as we have made it seem, then we need to ask ourselves some serious questions such as:

- To what extent will it continue to negatively impact human society?
- At what point will it stop getting worse?
- How bad will it get before most people realize that life should not be this way?

Many wealthy people are lost in the darkness of their industry. On the outside, it appears as though life could not be any better than their lavishly blessed existence, but on the inside, they are utterly empty, lonely, and sad. They often resort to heavy drug usage. They party hard, and yet, they are miserable. They shop more frequently than the average person and cannot seem to find joy in their possessions. Based on our idealized expectation of wealthy lives, one would think that the wealthy would be happier than the poor. However, happiness is a state of mind, as opposed to a purchasable product.

According to the implied promises of this world—implied through media outlets such as television and the internet—material possessions should augment one's quality of life, but they do not. Properties cannot make one joyful. A person can have everything one could ever ask for and lack joy. In this paragraph, I discussed two synonymous states of mind, happiness, and joyfulness. They may be used interchangeably, but they are indeed different experiences especially when we consider the joy that comes from God and the happiness we can find on earth.

The joy found in the LORD is greater than any bit of worldly happiness anyone can experience! Earthly happiness is merely the fleeting taste of contentment found in the temporal pleasures of life. We encounter such happiness when we do something fun or achieve something of value. The joy found in the LORD, however, is long-lasting contentment, which is not contingent upon the "worldly" things (wealth, possessions, popularity, good moments, etc.). It is found in the knowledge of the LORD, a relationship with Him, a fascination with the way He moves and operates in our lives, and the fulfillment of our purpose as we live our lives according to the good plans He has for us. Joy is the light that shines within us. It is a light that the dark world cannot comprehend. Some see it and are drawn to it while others see it and feel repulsed.

In recent years, many strange and disturbing events have occurred which indicate that sinister forces are at work in the world. Take, for instance, the Miami Cannibal Attack of 2012. Cannibalism in the public streets of a modern city should never have been a possibility at this point in human "evolution," yet, someone recorded a man feasting on another's face. This act was put to a stop when police officers shot and killed the cannibal. Toxicology reports were only able to find marijuana in the assailant's body, but no other drug that could have caused him to act so grotesquely.

There has been a plethora of other vile incidents such as mass murders, violent protests, etc. Even so, the Miami Cannibal attack gave those who were spiritually "awake" a glimpse into the spiritual component of this world. Believers in Yahweh (the God of the Bible) are not typically surprised by such evils. Sure, they are disturbing and horrific, but we understand that we do not wrestle against flesh and blood but powers and principalities. When one person hates another, the hate (he or she has within) is of spiritual origin. Either the person was exposed to hatred and grew to accept it, or a foreign spirit is at work in them.

Wandering spirits (called demons) can hijack a consenting host's body entirely or cohabit symbiotically. They can also do so without consent if the host is weak-willed. The earliest example of this was the Satan's use of a serpent's body in the garden of Eden. Almost everyone has probably heard of demonic possession, but it is not as rare as most would think. While there is no statistic to measure how many people are (or have been) possessed, live (or have lived) with demons, or even how many have been influenced by them, we know that evil entities exist in this realm. Though they are invisible, we can see the aftermath of their mischief.

In recent years, we have witnessed alleged enforcers of justice and law brutalize black brothers and sisters of our dysfunctional human family. They often harassed, intimidated, assaulted, and or killed their victims. We have also heard of good police officers who were killed by heartless people. Life was never supposed to be this messy! Chaos was in the beginning when the world was amorphous and void! Chaos was there when darkness was upon the face of the deep, and the spirit of the LORD moved upon the surface of the water before He spoke the famous first words, "Let there be light!" Now, however, in this realm, which the Bible says is ruled by the Satan, "the Prince of the Powers of the air," chaos is multiplying faster than Order is subjecting it.

We are approaching a worldwide culture that hearkens back to the days of Noah. Recall that before Adam and Eve sinned, God equipped them with every tool they needed to overcome and make the right choice, and then He was silent while they practiced the very self-determination that He created them to use. After they sinned by eating of the forbidden fruit, He visited them with judgment. Also recall that before Cain slew his brother, God equipped him with all the precautionary advice he would need to abort his angry course; then, the LORD was silent as Cain practiced His self-determination. After Cain sinned, God visited him with the severe, yet merciful judgment which Cain did not deserve. During the time of Noah, God gave humankind what they needed to choose wisely. He even blessed them with a 120-year grace period. During that grace period, Noah warned as many people as he could. They laughed and scoffed while the LORD was silent, but then He came with judgment in the form of a flood, something no one at that time had ever seen.

As silent as God has been, He equipped us with all the tools to choose wisely in these last days. We have the Bible. We have access to God, our Heavenly Father, and Savior through Christ Jesus, yet the world is not taking full advantage of the grace of the LORD. So, one day, our loving God will return as Judge and Arbiter to an astonished world. He **will** judge *without bias or exception* for His grace was once available to all, but in the fullness of time, which He alone determined, there will be no more chances. If life was a test all along, then this will be the moment where our teacher says, "Class put your pens and pencils down." If life was a dream, this will be the moment when the loud alarm wakes us up. If life was a 'party at my house,' then God will be the parent who returns to see how we have trashed the home He built. And if life was a heist for some of the richest, and most powerful people who had made unlawful deals with dark entities—to become perpetrators and accomplices in iniquity or even silencers against the righteous, then they will understand in that day that God is officer, judge, jury, and executioner.

He is the LORD most High—El Elyon—far above any political or religious authority. Like it or not, He is above the entire host of Heaven, and He most certainly is above earth both literally and figuratively. Master of strategy, reconnaissance, and even war, He will always hold the high ground. In other words, it is and forever will be **impossible** to subdue Him! Despite His tremendous love for us, Romans 2:6 says He will render to every man according to his deeds (women are included in this). In the days of Noah, He did something similar with the Great Flood. He brought judgment upon a corrupt world, but not before He showed grace and mercy.

CHAPTER 14

The Sacredness of Blood

After the Flood, God made a covenant with Noah, His family, and all human beings who had yet to be born.

Let us read Genesis 9:3-6 (KJV). We will begin with the third verse and analyze it.

3 Every moving thing that liveth shall be meat for you; even as the green herb have I given you all things.

Here, God permitted us to start eating meat. He made it clear in the following verses that we should not kill animals irresponsibly or unreasonably, nor should we consume the blood of the animal because its blood is sacred to Him. Blood is a catalyst for life. Our hearts must circulate blood throughout our bodies so that we may live. As our hearts beat, oxygenated blood is carried through our muscles and organs to keep the body "alive and well."

On an even more microscopic level, our cells travel through the bloodstream sustained by nutrients released into the blood. Important cells and even chemicals transit through it. Additionally, skin repair is made possible by the remarkable coagulation of blood. Hopefully, you get the idea. Most importantly, while this is beyond our current theoretical science, blood **may** be a conduit through which the energy of the spirit animates the flesh! Without blood, we are as inanimate as we would be without the Spirit of Life.

We lose blood continuously throughout our lives, but our bodies regenerate and replace it. It is one of the only substances that permeates and fills our entire bodies from head to toe! It occupies roughly the same space that the spirit is thought to hold. Why is that? —And why is it that electrochemical reactions within the body need that conductive medium?

Do you recall when I discussed the way the spirit interacts within the body? It is both the transmitter of life energy and the will as well as a receiver of information from the external world via the sensors in the body. From this reasoning, I dare to speculate that our ability as spiritual beings to interact with the physical world has a lot to do with this medium called blood. I further propose (and daringly so) that it is for this reason loss of blood results in a progressive loss of consciousness as the spirit gradually loses its bond with the flesh (muscles, tissues, etc.) but back to what God was telling Noah and the generations succeeding him

4 But flesh with the life thereof, which is the blood thereof, shall ye not eat.

(because blood is precious to God.)

5 And surely the blood of your lives will I require; at the hand of

every beast will I require it, and at the hand of man; at the hand of every man's brother will I require the life of man.

Consider blood as worth seven thousand times the price of its weight in gold (if not more) in God's sight. The loss of life grieves him as we saw when Cain killed his brother Abel. Recall how Abel's blood is said to have "cried out" to the LORD, compelling His vengeance upon Cain.

Henceforth the value which our Heavenly Father placed on blood was explicitly established for all generations. He promulgated a law of requital regarding life for life. Murderers will have to give account for every drop of blood they shed. If they escape punishment in this life, rest assured justice will find them in the next. Likewise, suicide (the murder of the self) is a misdeed that one must be held accountable for. After all, to kill the self, blood must be spilled, contaminated, or somehow tampered with to result in death to the body. The LORD, who promised to avenge the "blood of our souls," will hold any human accountable for accelerating his or her own demise. Our present reality must be endured and overcome with love, sincerity, and the pursuit of righteousness. It is indeed tough to live in this world, but the LORD wants us to overcome because through its trials, He teaches us virtues such as patience, forgiveness, and hope.

6 Whoso sheddeth man's blood, by man shall his blood be shed: for in the image of God made He man.

With this verse, He authorized civil government and law. Let's keep in mind that as much as society dislikes certain aspects of our imperfect and often dishonest governmental institutions (i.e., the lying politicians, the conspiracies and scandals), the concept of government, and the institution of it are critical to societal integrity. Structure is vital to everything; for, without it, things fall apart, whether we are referring to physical objects such as buildings or abstract subjects like the "fabric" of society, the integrity of a family, etc. In the absence of government, societal order devolves into full vagary. Therefore, God, who had executed judgment upon mankind, transferred that ability to deliver justice for a life taken. Even so, as with other things God has entrusted to us on earth, we abuse our power.

Innocents have lost their lives under death penalties solely based on suspicion or worse, pure hatred. Often-times, their lives were taken hours, days, or months before all evidence would have absolved them. Even governments on multiple levels (county, state, and federal) reflect the same vulnerability to vices that the very human beings comprising them also have. Although God commanded the establishment of governance by human beings, it is in observing man's rule (among other things) that we see the human susceptibility to stumble ever more clearly.

Society has seen that even presidents and kings can succumb to the lust of the flesh and partake in all types of debauchery. It has also witnessed how fear, anger, and greed can cause violent destabilization within nations. The world has seen rulers corrupted with power. As a result, we have learned that wherever there is power, corruption is near. This, of course, only applies in the sinful world of man.

Absolute power is said to corrupt absolutely, but I would like for us to understand that power itself does not corrupt. Rather, it brings out the deepest most hidden desires of the heart that we are otherwise too afraid to act upon and therefore hide from everyone else. Imagine, for instance, someone who is secretly racist. Without power, he can do nothing with his hate, but if he is empowered, suddenly he seems to behave like an entirely different person. His newly acquired position of power has not corrupted him nor transformed him. It has merely brought his hidden feelings and desires to light. It has made him bold.

A position of authority does not change a man. Rather in biblical prose, it can "harden his heart," meaning that it strengthens his resolve to act out his desires. What we see here is that power itself is not dangerous. The root of corruption is in the secret desire of the heart, which the word of the LORD says is continuously wicked.

I challenge you, dear reader, to monitor your own thoughts throughout the day, and indeed be honest with yourself. Are your thoughts pure throughout the day? Most of us would find that we think sinful thoughts at least once every day!

Influential people are no different. God knew that even our governmental institutions would be imperfect, but He legitimized them. One of the first steps that He took to endorse them was His postdiluvian laws of moral equity, namely life for life. He did not do this to promote vengeance. Instead, He sanctioned government to teach us accountability and justice especially for crimes like murder (for blood is precious to Him).

Murder, like other crimes, is wrong, but not because Homo-erectus discovered that killing his neighbors made him feel guilty. It is wrong because the LORD is displeased by it, deems it a wicked act that requires a heavy penalty, and He imprinted this upon our conscience. For this and other crimes, He granted human beings the right to preside over court trials to determine guilt and consequence according to the deed. In this manner, he was teaching us justice because He is just and wants us to follow in His ways. Furthermore, God has also been teaching us accountability; for one day, when the world stands before Him to give account, all will understand that we are on trial! Whether or not we are allowed in God's kingdom will have nothing to do with how rich or poor and disadvantaged we were, our intelligence, how much time we spent in quiet meditation, or how often we went to church. The Bible says we have only one mediator who can make us appear blameless before the perfectly Holy God of everything. That mediator is Jesus the Christ who shed His perfect blood about 2,000 years ago specifically to bear the punishment of our sins.

CHAPTER 15
God's Nature and the Imago Dei,

God is eternal, and His divine motive from everlasting is to enjoy perfect and harmonious fellowship with mankind. At the dawn of the concept of "Time" (as we know it), the LORD created both the Heavens and the earth. Nothing existed before Him, but everything that was brought forth emerged from Him as He is the source of all, but why?

God is perfect and self-sufficient alone. Even so, from everlasting, He loved us so much and proved it through an unfathomably great sacrifice. God suffered for us and was tortured to death to redeem humanity. In the beginning, when He created us, He distinguished us from all other life forms by making us in His likeness.

Many theologians and believers currently agree that human beings are tripartite. To them, the "Imago Dei" (Latin for "image of God") implies tripartism of body, soul, and spirit. These theologians suggest that this supposed tripartism corresponds to the "Holy Trinity of God," for they imagine Him to be three persons comprising the "godhead" —Father, Son, and Holy Spirit. God, however, does not consist of a Trinity. There are many verses in scripture that support this fact. Isaiah 44:6 and Deuteronomy 6:4 are two such examples. Though it is not impossible for Yahweh, "the Great I AM" to be anything, He chooses to be, He is not three persons, and certainly not three in one. His Holy Spirit is in every believer simultaneously, and yet, God in His full glory resides in Heaven! How can this be?

The Bible teaches us that God is Spirit. Therefore, if the "Holy Spirit" is in us (on earth), yet we know our Heavenly Father (God) is Spirit, then who and what is in Heaven—an unholy Spirit? A not-quite-as-Holy Spirit? It would be unbiblical to think the Holy Spirit dwells in born-again believers, yet the Spirit we call "our Father in Heaven" is a different Holy Spirit. Do you see how the Trinitarian doctrine can get weird? It overcomplicates something that is actually much simpler. That is not to say we can ever fathom God, but those who have a relationship with Him are supposed to know Him and understand all He has revealed to us about His nature.

"Hear O Israel, the LORD our God is one". The Book of John reveals that in the Beginning, a being He calls "the Word" existed and it created heaven and earth, and in the Beginning. The Word was with God, and The Word was God. Without this Word, nothing was created. This same Word, which was also God, became flesh and dwelt among us as ImmanuEL (God with us). The prophet Isaiah foretold (under the inspiration of the Holy Spirit) that unto us (Jews and gentiles), a child would be born, and the government would be upon His shoulders. "His name would be called Wonderful, Counselor, **The Mighty God**, The **Everlasting Father**." Isaiah was (of course) referring to Jesus the Messiah; and when Jesus grew into a man, He one day admitted to having seen Abraham (an ancient ancestor). The people around Him were appalled by what they thought was a lie. They replied, "but you're not even fifty, and you say you've seen Abraham?" Then Jesus answered, "To be completely honest with you, before Abraham was, I AM."

Anyone who has thoroughly read through the old testament knows that God revealed Himself to Moses as "Ehyeh" (the first-person form of the verb "Hayah" meaning "to be"). Only God could call Himself "Ehyeh" ("I AM") in the sense of "I always exist, therefore, eternal is what I am," but people would learn to call Him "Yahweh," simply meaning "He is." In the new testament, Jesus showed His divinity through miracles. They were deliberate demonstrations of His dominion over creation, for only the creator of the world would have power over everything in it! He calmed a storm to show His sovereignty over nature and her elements. Jesus walked on water to prove He could defy the laws of physics (the very laws He had built into reality). He healed all diseases to show that even if all else has failed, God has the power to restore health. He resurrected the dead, showing He has power over life and death. He transformed food and drink demonstrating He not only created what we ingest, but could manipulate it, and so much more! Additionally, Jesus is said to be the image of the invisible God, who is Spirit.

Do you remember when I said that our spirits are invisible even to our persons? When we look in a mirror, we can only see the shells housing our spirits, but not our spirits themselves? Well, Christ is the image of God. He is the invisible spirit of God in visible flesh. God is Spirit. Yet Christ, while on earth, was the fullness of God in a human body designed to die for the atonement of sins so that whoever would choose to believe in Him would be shown mercy by the same God who not only created them but loves them dearly. Whoever has seen Christ has seen the merciful and Everlasting Father. With that said, when Christ ascended, He sent the very spirit who was in Him to all believers who give their lives to Him. That Holy Spirit is the Spirit of Christ who now dwells within those who accept Christ Jesus as their savior. Do you understand?

So, when we are told to baptize in the name of the Father and the Son and the Holy Spirit, we are not to baptize as people who do not know the LORD is one God. We should not baptize with vain repetition of "in the name of the Father, Son, and Holy Spirit" and make a gesture of the cross. Instead, since we know that name, we should baptize in the **name** (singular) they all share. It is the name that has been exalted above every other name; —JESUS who made heaven and earth. He is the same God who promised Adam and Eve He would return in the form of one of their descendants to defeat the Satan and redeem us from sin! His Hebrew name is Yeshua (for He is Salvation or as He alone is worthy to say, "I AM Salvation"). As a matter of fact, the prophet John recorded in the book of Revelation, that Christ spoke to the world saying "I am the alpha and omega, the first and the last." Who else can say that, but God?!

The trinitarian doctrine suggests God consists of the Father, Son, and Holy Spirit. It is not far from the truth, but it is inaccurate enough to be deceptive. The Bible indeed mentions these three forms of God (especially where it instructs people in the ritual of baptism as mentioned earlier; c.f. Matt 28:19), but they are not to be taken as three separate persons or three entities in one. We know the Son of God was born in the form of a man, but God is spirit. Therefore, if we exclude the Son (for the sake of a simple illustration), could we say that the Father and the Holy Spirit are one? Absolutely! They are the same! Our Heavenly Father is Spirit. He is a righteous and Holy Spirit?

Jesus referred to God in Heaven as "Father" because Jesus (*the man*) **was born**. Yet God Himself, who was in Heaven was also in Christ such that He was the fullness of God among men (EmmanuEL). Before Jesus was conceived in his mother Mary's womb, the Supreme and Holy Spirit of Life (whom we regard as our Heavenly Father and God), overshadowed Mary, then breathed Himself into Jesus like unto how He had breathed life into Adam. At that moment, fetal Jesus came alive. Though Jesus is also fully God, the Father calls Him "Son." God also calls Jesus, whom the Bible establishes as His Son, "God" and "Lord" (in Hebrews 1:8-12)! Just as striking is how the Almighty God gives Jesus credit in that same passage for the creation of the world. John 1:1-14, also clarifies that Jesus created the world, and was God before He was born in the form of a human.

As a result of the Trinitarian doctrine, many have falsely deduced that the meaning of Genesis 1:26 was that God created man in three parts body, soul, and spirit. It is time to shatter yet another misconception. In one of the previous chapters, I had, to an extent, demystified the spirit, body, and soul. Here, I will clarify their fundamental and relative natures.

Contrary to popular philosophy, we do not consist of three existential layers called body, spirit, and soul. Rather, we are spirit (which was breathed into flesh) and body (wherein is the Spirit of Life that was breathed into it). In Genesis, The Bible states that man became a living soul only after God breathed His spirit into him. *"And the LORD God formed man of the dust of the ground and breathed into his nostrils the breath of life; and man became a living soul."* -Genesis 2:7.

There are two aspects of our being that we and everyone else can recognize. The first is our physical appearance, and the second is our inner self, which is primarily spiritual essence. Though it is invisible, the spirit (our true person) when combined with the body and its visible actions and reactions creates the visible *'human being'* as opposed to the mere form of one.

The **product (or sum)** of the spirit-body union is the soul, which is the living (and conscious) creature. Man, therefore, is not truly "tri-partite" although he embodies a three-part equation. This fact is supported by God's written word in Ecclesiastes 12:7 which reads, "Then shall the dust return to the earth as it was: and the spirit shall return unto God who gave it." In this verse, we do not see a movement of three parts, but only two. The dust returns to the earth, and the spirit returns to God, for without a spirit living within the "dust," there is no soul (Hebrew "nephesh"). God explained who the dust was in Genesis 3:19 when He pronounced Adam's punishment. "In the sweat of your face shall you eat bread, till you return unto the ground; for out of it were you taken: for dust you are, and unto dust shall you return."

Human beings made in the likeness of God resemble the very God who often describes Himself using anthropomorphisms. "Jesus is the image (*or visible representation*) of the invisible God (*for God is spirit*)," according to Colossians 1:15; and according to Ephesians 4:4, "speaking of God, there is one body (Jesus) and one spirit (the Holy Spirit)." When God overshadowed Mary and breathed His Holy Spirit into the fetal Jesus, our Savior became the living, visible God born among humankind to die for our sins and rise three days later in victory over sin and death. Before that, however, God occasionally visited people in the Bible in glorified, but human-like forms, such as Melchizedek, who was said to be immortal! Christ was a different model whose body was engineered for worldwide salvation through death and resurrection. His blood had to be shed because the penalty for sin is death.

Nowadays, the phrase "body of Christ" is more often used to describe the church. Contrary to what many would believe, however, the church has never been a physical building. That is a lie from the Enemy who incorrectly took Christ's figurative language literally. God is not the author of confusion, but the Satan certainly is. When Jesus said He would destroy the temple and rebuild it in three days, the Enemy thought he knew God's plans. He believed Jesus would destroy the temple in Jerusalem. Since the Holy Spirit (the spirit that provides spiritual discernment) was not in the Pharisees who were against Jesus, his bold declaration was taken literally and triggered their anger. Little did they know, however, that Jesus was referring to his body and not a man-made temple.

Nowadays, the church has been mistaken for a physical building when it truly represents the congregation of believers all over the world. In the book of Acts, the Holy Spirit fills the place where the substitute body of Christ (the church) has assembled. From that moment on, the church became alive! It became a living soul (in a sense)!

With that said, and with these examples in mind, we can represent our physical composition with the following formula:

$$1 \text{ BODY} + 1 \text{ SPIRIT} = 1 \text{ LIVING SOUL}$$
$$\text{Just as}$$
$$1 \text{ PATTY} + 1 \text{ SLICED BUN} = 1 \text{ BURGER}$$

This equation is indeed tripartite, but man (as the living soul) is bipartite. He is a body that is animated by a spirit. According to James 2:26, "the body without the spirit is dead" the soul, therefore, can again be explained as the visibly living and conscious creature animated by the invisible life force, which we call our spirit. The spirit itself is made visible on this physical plane of existence by interfacing with a physical body. Only then does it become a soul. Furthermore, if we examine every passage from the Bible in which a soul is discussed, we can substitute that word with "being" or "consciousness," and it still retains its meaning.

As a result of the body, soul, and spirit misconception, many believers and theologians have misunderstood the Imago Dei. Though the book of Genesis zooms into the creation of mankind, focusing more on that event than the formation of other creatures, animals had been produced similarly! They, too, were brought forth from the earth, and God also breathed His spirit (the Spirit of Life) into them. The following excerpt supports this truth:

"And all flesh died that moved upon the earth, both of fowl, and cattle, and of beast, and of every creeping thing that creeps upon the earth, and even mankind. **_All_** in whose nostrils was the breath of life" Genesis 7:21-22.

So, if animals also have the "breath of life" in them (or a spirit), then they are living souls according to the soul equation that I shared a few paragraphs ago!! They are BODY + SPIRIT. To further drive and support this point, the original transcriptions of the Bible have used the Hebrew word "nephesh," which means "soul" for animals! With that said, one cannot suggest that being made in the image of God implies having body, spirit, and soul, as that would mean animals were also made in His image. We know this to be false. Instead, when God created man after His image and likeness ("made" in this case meaning "fashioned and appointed"), it had **nothing** to do with body, spirit, and soul. Instead, we are unique because we were made for the following purposes:

1. To have a close relationship with Him (as royal priests and His children)
2. To share dominion with Him on earth (as a President and Vice President, husband and wife would share authority. Obviously, God's ultimate will supersedes everything.)
3. To take care of His creation (stewardship)
4. To learn to design things also.

Animals do not meet those four qualifications! Therefore, when God said Let us make man in our image, He was pre-appointing humankind for those four roles mentioned above and showing humanity for generations to come that we had been chosen to be His representatives on earth to all living things. If a President is absent from a place, the Vice President is the image of His superior until the President returns. A Vice President has a special relationship with the President, the President shares authority with him, and the Vice President also takes care of any Presidential business when the President is away. Thus, when we were made in the image of God, we were made into rulers over all life on Earth. Our only Superior (in this realm) was the creator of it—the LORD God. We were the similitude of God to all other life forms just as Jesus is the image of the invisible God to us. Those who have seen Jesus, have seen our Father God, just as those who see our living bodies can see our invisible attributes through us.

CHAPTER 16
No Greater Love

As mentioned in my first book, "The Serpent's Lie," much to the shock and disappointment of many believers (hopefully, they have recuperated by now), God's six-day creation was not "perfect" by itself. That has been a huge misconception! Nothing in the Genesis account is said to have been created "perfect" (in any of the existing translations), although, to this day, many preachers may spread this unsupported fallacy!

Had God made everything "perfect," He would have said so. Instead, He saw they were "good" and "very good." For anyone who believes that everything was once "perfect" simply because God is perfect, I pose the following questions:

Why would Adam have had to maintain a perfect garden? Would not trees, grass, and fruit all grow in perfect size and quantity?

God delegated to Adam the responsibility of "dressing" and caring for the garden in which He had placed him. Therefore, work was needed to maintain its "goodness." Thus, as magnificent as their realm had been, God speaks truly in His word. If He calls something "perfect," then it is "perfect," and if He calls something "good" or "very good," it is precisely as He said. The only entirely perfect thing, according to the Bible, is God Himself. That is to say that He and everything about Him is flawless in EVERY way (I.e.,

His nature, His plans, His power, His knowledge, etc.). If we ever dare to consider the earth and all life upon it to have once been perfect, we must also acknowledge that this could **only** have been the case ***while* they existed in willful submission to the Creator**. Nothing apart from God is perfect (on its own).

Even when the LORD described one of His most beautiful creatures in the Bible, Helel Ben Sachar (the one the world knows as "Lucifer" and the Satan), He stated:

"You were the seal of perfection, full of wisdom, and perfect in beauty."

In other words, the Satan did not symbolize "perfection" (itself), but He was the "emblem", seal, or stamp of perfection. An emblem such as one used by a well-known brand can be a symbol of excellent quality, but the brand itself does not *mean* "quality." Instead, its perceived quality is derived from an association between the product and the **reputation** of its maker. The Satan bore light and beauty, two aspects of the LORD that filled him with sinful pride. The "seal of perfection," which in a sense was a signature of God, manifested itself through Lucifer in the following two areas:

he was "full of wisdom

and

he was perfect ***in beauty***."

Skipping forward a bit, God goes on to say (about the Satan):

You were perfect in your ways from the day that you were created, till iniquity was found in you." -Ezekiel 28: 15

In other words, the Satan was once perfect (in the context of being flawlessly exemplary or blameless) ***in his ways until*** sin was found in him. He was not perfect in might or power, perfect in wisdom, virtue, grace, patience, and humility. He was only perfect in beauty and his ways or deeds (only for a short while)—until sin showed itself in him through unbridled pride and lust for power.

Here we can glimpse how perfection in some areas ruined a being who ignored the fact that God was His source and therefore deserves supremacy forever. Lucifer may have been ideal in some areas. However, he was clearly imperfect in humility, contentment, and other areas. He wanted to possess the glory and power of the Highest! The Satan felt he was good enough to be God, and he did not want to be anything less than an equal.

Thankfully, the LORD did not create humankind to be perfect. He wants to perfect us in due time (in the specific areas in which we are destined to excel), but man was not created perfect. We were only made after His likeness.

After eating from the forbidden fruit, humanity became more like God (in the sense of **_knowing good and evil_**), and we can see the effects. Knowledge alone can ruin many. To make matters worse, our disobedience continues to separate us from a relationship with God, for we often believe that "we know best." We pursue and glorify knowledge (as long as it avoids God) and we exalt those who have the kind of knowledge we seek.

The LORD desires to improve us daily. Had man already been created "perfect" in knowledge and power, then knowing the outcome of every scenario, understanding all things, and having the ability to do all would have made human beings feel self-sufficient. What place would God ever have had in our lives if we lacked nothing? Do you ever hunger immediately after your stomach has been filled? Of course not! Why do you need food if you are stuffed full of it? What does one single dollar matter to someone richer than you can imagine? Likewise, if we had the power to obtain everything we could desire, on our own, how much would a relationship with the LORD or anyone else matter to us?

I believe that we all have a spiritual dependence on God (whether we know it or not). He is the only one who can fulfill the direct needs of our spirits. That is why I also believe that we all naturally seek, have sought, or will seek Him at one point or another (whether we realize what exactly we are looking for). Our spirits, (which originate from God) desire to draw nearer to Him but our pride can significantly hinder us if we are not careful.

There is a fulfillment that only God can provide, and He wants to do so. There are, however, many interceptors, distractions, and gateways that can cause us to lose our way. For instance, while trying to escape sorrow, regret, and anxiety, many people resort to drugs, drinking, pornography, etc. Others look for a way, a truth, and a natural, secular "joie de vivre" (joy of life/living). The truth is that their spirits truly hunger for a relationship with God. But just as junk foods can temporarily replace a hearty meal (to the detriment of the body), there are false substitutes to God. A spirit can be temporarily satisfied with the false promise that it is getting closer to the truth. Ultimately, however, it will be disappointed if it neglects the one true God.

God wants us to know that He experienced life as a human being. He wants us to come to Him. God does not expect us to be perfect but does expect us to recognize Him as the ideal to strive toward. After all, He lived a sinless life as Christ.

If the North Star changed its position in the night sky, it would be unreliable for navigation. If straight edges ceased to be straight, how would one draw a neat line? If there were no standards, goals, or ideals, what would we aspire toward? And if there were no boundaries, what would we indulge in and refrain from? The LORD has always been and will always be the perfect mold to model ourselves after.

We all seek Him at one point or another. How many times have we searched for the "meaning of life," our purpose, fulfillment, joy, freedom, adventure, stability, knowledge, wisdom, truth, forgiveness, redemption, or a way out of our current hardship?

When our spirits have been stirred enough, we start to recognize our desire for the extraordinary, which can take us to various places. Much like a compass, our spirits tug us in the right direction (toward God). However, without turn by turn navigation, we can still become lost in a labyrinth of corridors (even with a compass). One path might promise self-fulfillment through pure empty-minded meditation. Another might promise it through monasticism, self-denial, and sacrifice to achieve enlightenment or "earn" salvation. Still, others might promise it by empowering us to seek "the god within." People who buy into these false doctrines of righteous living tend to perceive themselves as good if they do good things, but no one is a "good person" (by nature). Some have done worse things than others, but we **all** have sinned and fallen short

I am not suggesting that we go around brooding. Instead, the point that I want to drive is that we are not the ultimate deciders of what qualifies as "good" and "bad." We never were...

Those who have been redeemed in Christ are not better than the lost. They have simply taken hold of a gift from God who loves us enough to have died for us in the form of Jesus the Christ. That was the Divine Motive that Jesus (who was simultaneously God in a mortal body) would come to the very earth that He had created so that He could shed His blood for us. He would do this for all who had sinned and proven themselves worthy of death just as Adam and Eve had done.

The penalty for sin is death, but Jesus Christ came and died for us to obtain grace and salvation. The choice is ours to receive His gift. For even as His created likeness, any man or woman who has not accepted His gift of salvation, is at risk of eternal regret. He does not desire for us to remain lost, but to take advantage of His mercy. Love lacks value when it is forced. It is for this reason that God has given us the gift of free will. The wages of sin may be certain death, but the gift of God is eternal life through Jesus Christ our Lord. So, what will you choose today?

A Message to the Reader:

If you enjoyed this book, please share it with your friends and family. Writing it was an incredible mental and spiritual journey for me and I sincerely hope it strengthened your faith in our true and living God. I believe firmly that we serve one who rewards those who diligently seek Him (as Hebrews 11:6 says).

Thank you for embarking on this journey with me. I look forward to many more journeys with you. In the meantime, I do blog as well, so feel free to visit the following website:

www.mysoulhaven.com

With respect to my next book, rest assured, dear reader, I am working tirelessly on the next project as Christ gives me strength.

May the LORD bless you abundantly.

-Miguel A. Valembrun Jr.

Copyright © 2020 Miguel A. Valembrun Jr.

All rights reserved.

ISBN: 978-1-950773-02-2

MAV JR.

www.ingramcontent.com/pod-product-compliance
Lightning Source LLC
Chambersburg PA
CBHW032124090426
42743CB00007B/458